Christianity, Islam, and the West

Robert A. Burns

UNIVERSITY PRESS OF AMERICA,® INC.
Lanham • Boulder • New York • Toronto • Plymouth, UK

Copyright © 2011 by
University Press of America,® Inc.
4501 Forbes Boulevard
Suite 200
Lanham, Maryland 20706
UPA Acquisitions Department (301) 459-3366

Estover Road
Plymouth PL6 7PY
United Kingdom

Library of Congress Control Number: 2011926390
ISBN: 978-0-7618-5559-0 (paperback : alk. paper)
eISBN: 978-0-7618-5560-6

∞^{TM} The paper used in this publication meets the minimum
requirements of American National Standard for Information
Sciences—Permanence of Paper for Printed Library Materials,
ANSI Z39.48-1992

Contents

Preface

This book has its origin in a course I have taught at the University of Arizona for some thirty years. The course is entitled "Comparative Religions" and deals with the history and teachings of the Abrahamic religions: Judaism, Christianity, and Islam. Those who have enrolled in the class have come from diverse religious and cultural backgrounds. Whatever the mix, there has been a shared curiosity about all three religions, but since the attack of 9/11 on the World Trade Center, the students are especially interested in Islam. Like most Americans, they have little or no knowledge of the Islamic religion.

This book deals briefly with the origin and main teachings of the Islamic religion. It then discusses the kind of questions asked of me most frequently. Hopefully, this approach will be helpful not only when used in courses in comparative religions, but will be useful to study groups and to other interested individuals as well. The glossary of technical words and the selected bibliography ("Further Reading") should also be an aid to the reader.

In putting together a book of this scope, acknowledgement of those whose work I have drawn from could be almost endless. Hopefully the textual references given throughout the book indicate sufficiently my debt to the scholars who have influenced my thinking.

Introduction

Relations between Christianity and the Islam have been mutually hostile for centuries. From the 7th through the 15th century there were Muslim invasions of The Holy Land, Central Europe, Italy, Spain, and North Africa. Christians reacted principally through the Crusades (1095-1291) which resulted in anti-Christian attitudes among Muslims. At the same time, Christian disdain toward Islam intensified. Throughout the following centuries, very few Christians have had an authentic knowledge of Islam and such has been true of Islam vis-à-vis Christianity.

The 19th century and the historical studies of Islam which it produced paved the way for a less polemical assessment of Islam on the part of Christian theology. Nevertheless, colonialism (the domination of much of the Islamic world by European powers from the 17th through the 20th century) and the military, economic, cultural, and religious expansion of the West during the past two centuries, has led to greater hostility on the part of the Islamic world. Mutual understanding and dialogue, for the most part, has come to a standstill.

Misinformation about Islam, and for that matter, sheer ignorance, is common today in the United States. The purpose of this book is to help alleviate this problem. Dialogue between the two religions, which hopefully will bring mutual understanding and respect, is a necessity if world peace is to be attained. Roman Catholicism at the Second Vatican Council (1962-1965) encouraged such dialogue in the "Declaration on the Relationship of the Church to Non-Christian Religions" by urging Catholics and Muslims "to forget the past and to strive sincerely for mutual understanding," making "common cause for safeguarding and fostering social justice, moral values, peace and freedom."[1] Other Christian communities have stated similar ideas. As a result, a number of interfaith conferences have been held but unfortunately have reached very few adherents on either side.

On October 17th, 2007, a letter signed by 138 Muslim leaders was sent to Pope Benedict XVI and other Christian leaders throughout the world, calling for dialogue between the two religions for the sake of world peace. In addition to the Pope, who accepted the invitation, the letter is addressed to all of the Eastern Orthodox Church, the Calcedonian and pre-Calcedonian Churches, to many Protestant Churches, and to the World Council of Churches. Many accepted this invitation.

Common ground for this dialogue, which began in November 2008, is rooted in the twofold commandment to love God and one's neighbor. As the dialogue unfolds, it will be based on respect for every human person, an objective knowledge of one another's religion without downplaying differences, and on a commitment to promote mutual respect for one another. When this occurs, Muslims and Christians can begin to work together to promote justice and peace throughout the world. The attack on the World Trade Center on September 11th, 2001, the war in Afghanistan, the situation in Iraq and elsewhere in the Middle East, confirm the urgent need for such dialogue. Since this book is intended primarily for a Christian readership, an introduction to Islam and its teachings will be presented. Included in this study will be an examination of commonalities and differences between the two religions and other factors which must be understood if a true dialogue is to occur. In regard to this, the results of the Gallup World Poll as found in *Who Speaks For Islam? What a Billion Muslims Really Think* by John L. Esposito and Salia Magahed, will be used as a vital source throughout this book once a brief introduction to Islam has been presented.[2]

NOTES

1. "The Dogmatic Constitution on the Church," in Walter Abbot, ed., *The Documents of Vatican II* (New York: Herder, 1966).

2. John L. Esposito and Salia Magahed, *Who Speaks for Islam? What a Billion Muslims Really Think* (New York: Gallup Press, 2007).

Part I

THE ISLAMIC RELIGION

Chapter One

Muhammad and the Qur'an

Muhammad was born in 570 in the city of Mecca. He was a member of the powerful Quraysh tribe. His clan, the Hashim, was not prominent but it was well regarded. His father, Banu Hashim, died before he was born and his mother died when he was six, perhaps even earlier. He was raised by his grandfather, Abd al-Muttalib, who acted as his guardian, but died two years later. His uncle, Abu Talib, then became his guardian. In his youth, Muhammad was a shepherd but later worked in the caravan trade. In his twenties he worked for a wealthy woman, a widow named Khadijah, as a manager of her caravan. Muhammad and Khadijah married in 595. He was twenty-five and she is said to have been forty. However, it is possible she was somewhat younger since she and Muhammad had six children, four daughters and two sons. Neither of the sons survived childhood.

Muhammad's call to be a prophet occurred in 610. This took place in a cave on Mt. Hira, near the city of Mecca. Muhammad had often gone there to pray and meditate. He was always a spiritual person. The angel Gabriel appeared to him and told him he was to be the messenger of God. He was told to "recite" the revelation he received. Qur'an means "recitation" in Arabic. Muhammad, who was illiterate, served as God's intermediary. Muslims believe that the Qur'an is the literal word of God. From 610 until his death in 632, a period of twenty-three years, Muhammad continued to receive revelations. During this time, the Qur'an's 114 chapters (called suras) were revealed to him. Muslims believe the Qur'an was preserved in oral and written form during the lifetime of Muhammad. The entire text was collected into an official standardized text during the reign of the caliph Uthman (644-656). In length, the Qur'an is approximately four-fifths the size of the New Testament. For Muslims, the Qur'an is entirely God's word except for its arrangement, verse numbering, and the names of the surahs (chapters) which were produced after Muhammad's death.

The Qur'an is arranged from the longest to the shortest sura without a chronological structure. The exceptions to this arrangement is the short opening sura, "Al Fatihah," which is the most common prayer of the Muslim tradition and is repeated by Muslims every day. It reads:

In the name of God, Most gracious, Most merciful.
Praise be to God, the Cherisher and Sustainer of the worlds;
Most Gracious, Most Merciful;
Master of the Day of Judgment.
Thee do we worship and Thine aid we seek.
Show us the straight path,
The way of those on whom Thou hast bestowed Thy grace,
Those whose portion is not wrath,
And who go not astray.[1]

Muslims believe that the Qur'an, as well as the Torah and the Gospels, is based on a tablet written in Arabic that exists in heaven. Regardless of their native language, Muslims memorize and recite the Qur'an in Arabic since it was revealed in this way. Until modern times, the Qur'an was published only in Arabic. Translations, seen by Muslims as "interpretations," usually have the Arabic text printed alongside. It is believed that it is impossible to translate the Qur'an in its reality into another language. Translations are therefore unusable for ritual and liturgical purposes. The sound of the Arabic in the Qur'an, with its rhythmic power, is experienced as numinous.

Muhammad began his preaching in 613. He preached a message of social justice and the need to help the poor, orphans, and the weak. His teaching was not welcomed by those in power and the wealthy. The message was accompanied by the threat of condemnation. Sura 104:1-3 states: "Woe unto him who amasses wealth and counts it as a safeguard, thinking that his wealth will make him live forever." At the beginning, his message was accepted by very few. His wife Khadijah was the first to become a Muslim. Early followers included his cousin and son-in-law, Ali, and Abu Bakr. Both were later to become successors (caliphs) of Muhammad, though Shi'ites (who will be discussed in a later chapter) accepted only Ali.

Muhammad's preaching included resurrection of the body at the end of history and a final judgment. Those deemed worthy would be rewarded in heaven and those who were unworthy would suffer in hell. These teachings were met with great ridicule. According to the Qu'ran, the "Day of Judgment: is the "Day of Reckoning." On the last day of human history, the graves will be opened and the dead will rise to life. God is the universal judge and the last judgment is ushered in on the sound of trumpets and horns and by cosmic catastrophes: seas will overflow, the sun will be darkened, and clouds will fall from heaven (Suras 56:1-7; 69:13-16; 77:8-13; 78:18-20; 81:1-14; 82:1-5; 84:1-6). God will open the Book of Life in which all good and evil deeds are listed. The Qur'an describes both heaven (Paradise) and hell in very concrete terms. In heaven, the just will be granted great happiness, a life of untroubled sensual joy. They may even enjoy the company of charming, untouched paradisical virgins (houris) who are "companions pure, most beautiful of eye." The description of hell is also quite vivid. Hell is usually referred to as "fire" and sometimes as "Gehenna." The damned will suffer "hell-fire scorching the skin" (Sura 74:27-29), for whom a food is prepared "that chokes" (Sura 73:13); they must eat from the tree whose fruit is "like molten lead" and will "boil in the belly" (Suras 44:43-46; 37:62-68; 56:51-56).

Above all, Muhammad's teaching that there is only one God (Allah) caused many to revile him. The Quraysh tribe to which he belonged controlled the Ka'bah, a cubic-shaped building surrounded by 360 idols representing forces of nature and heavenly beings. Every Arab tribe could find its deities there and religious pilgrimages were combined with caravans organized for trade in Mecca. The Quraysh had considerable status among the Arabs for their stewardship of this sacred building, and they benefitted greatly economically from the pilgrims and traders who came to Mecca to perform religious rituals and business activities. Muhammad's teaching that there is only one God, the God of Abraham, threatened the religious practices and business attracted by the pilgrimages to the Ka'bah. At stake were Mecca's financial and economic systems as well as its existing religious, social, and political institutions. In fact, the inner unity and external prestige of the tribe itself was threatened.

The message of the Qur'an and of Muhammad's presentation of that message included not only belief in the one God but the demand of moral behavior from its creatures. God's mercy is also emphasized as is his justice. Nonetheless, the Meccans saw the teachings of Muhammad as a serious threat to the status quo and did all they could to oppose him. By 615, the situation became increasingly dangerous and Muhammad recommended that some of his followers should emigrate to Christian Ethiopia for a time. Eighty-nine men and eighteen women are said to have done so and evidently were received with a friendly welcome. The year 619 brought great sadness to Muhammad when his wife, Khadijah, and his uncle, Abu Talib, died. Abu Talib, who never became a Muslim, was nevertheless Muhammad's obligatory protection. He now had no political support and the Muslim community probably numbered little more than one hundred members.

In 620, Muhammad met with twelve delegates from Medina and a year later with others from that city. They were impressed by Muhammad's leadership skills. In 622, seventy-three men from Medina took oaths that they would practice Islam and obey Muhammad. Some sort of stable government was needed in their city, and they believed Muhammad could provide the needed leadership. The same year, Muhammad asked his followers in Mecca to emigrate to Medina, which was about one hundred and eighty miles north of Mecca. They did so in small groups totaling about seventy-five Muslims. Mecca had become so dangerous that Muhammad and his chief assistant, Abu Bakr, moved by back roads to Medina, arriving there on September 24th, 622. This episode is called the Hijrah (emigration, not flight) of the prophet and his followers. A community of faith was established. Year one of the Muslim calendar begins in 622.

In Medina, Muhammad was successful in reconciling two warring pagan tribes who eventually became Muslim. Three Jewish tribes (all of whom were Arab), who resided in Medina, rejected Muhammad's religious claims and so became politically suspect to the prophet, and in military terms were not considered reliable in the battle with the Meccans who continued to strongly oppose the new Muslim community. The Jewish tribes did not want to be members of the Muslim confederation. As a results, Muhammad expelled the Jewish tribes one at a time.

What is known as the "Constitution of Medina" was produced over a number of years. It laid out the organization and structure of the new religious community. As Frederich Mattewson Denny writes:

> The remarkable thing about the Constitution of Medina is that it transformed Yathrib's (Medina's) warring and fractious tribes and clans into a kind of super-tribe, bound together not by kinship but by a common religious faith. This was a revolution in the social and political history of Arabia and made possible the eventual unification of the whole peninsula under the banner of Islam.[2]

Following the establishment of Islam in Medina, a number of battles were fought, some of which were quite important, others not; some were victorious, others not. But Islam continued to attract many followers and in 630, Muhammad led an army of 10,000 men into Mecca and captured the city without any real opposition. It was basically a bloodless conquest. One of the first things Muhammad did was to cleanse the Ka'bah of its 360 idols and rededicate it to Allah, the God of Abraham.

The Ka'bah is the most sacred shrine in the Islamic world. It is located inside the compound of the Grand Mosque in Mecca. "Ka'bah" is translated "cube" and it is a cube-shaped building known as the "House of God." It is draped over with a woven black cloth (the Kiswah), at the top of which are verses from the Qur'an embroidered in gold. The Ka'bah is said, by some, to have been originally built by Adam but it was destroyed over time and was later rebuilt by Abraham and his son, Ishmael. It is understood to replicate the heavenly "House of God" which contains the divine throne which is circumambulated by the angels. This heavenly ritual is reenacted during the pilgrimage to Mecca (the Hajj) by pilgrims who circumambulate the Ka'bah seven times, which is understood as symbolizing their entry before the presence of God. The Ka'bah contains the sacred Black Stone which is a meteorite believed to have been put into a corner of the building by Abraham and Ishmael. It is a symbol of God's covenant with the two of them and by extension with the entire Muslim community.

By the time of Muhammad's death in June 632, all Arabia was united by the religion of Islam. Shortly before his death, Muhammad led a pilgrimage to the Ka'bah and in his farewell sermon, which was delivered from a hill overlooking the plain of 'Arafat, he recited God's words:

> Today I have perfected your religion for you, and I have completed My blessing upon you, and I have approved Islam for your religion. (Sura 5:3)

NOTES

1. Yusuf Ali, ed., *The Holy Quran* (Brentwood, Marhland, Amana Corporation: 1987).

2. Frederich Mattewson Denny, *Introduction to Islam* (Upper Saddle River, New Jersey: Pearson Education, Inc., 2006).

Chapter Two

The Sunnis and the Shi'ites

Sunni and Shi'ite Muslims represent the two largest divisions in Islam. The Sunnis are approximately 85 percent of the Muslim population and the Shi'ites make up 15 percent. According to the 2008 edition of the *World Almanac*, there are 1,335,964,110 Muslims worldwide, which makes it the world's largest religion according to Monsignor Vitorio Formenti, in an interview with the Vatican newspaper *L'Osservatore Romano*. He said that Catholics, who are now the second largest religion, account for 17.4 percent of the world population, while Muslims are 19.2 percent. However, when all Christians are considered, they number over two billion. All Muslims share many beliefs and practices such as belief in one God, the role of Muhammad, the revelation of the Qur'an, and the five pillars of Islam (which will be discussed later). But like all religions, Islam has developed divisions and sects as well as schools of thought over religious and political issues of leadership, theology, the meaning of Islamic law, and responses to the West and modernity.

The split between the two groups can be traced to Muhammad's death in 632. The Sunnis, the followers of the Sunna (example) of Muhammad, who see themselves as the traditionalists of the community, believe the prophet died without designating a successor. They believe that leadership should be given to the most qualified person as chosen by the consensus of the community and not by hereditary succession, as is the position of the Shi'ites. The first successors of Muhammad, the "Four rightly guided caliphs" were Abu Bakr (632-634), 'Umar ibn al-Khattab (634-644), 'Uthman ibn 'Affan (644-665), and 'Ali ibn Abi Talib (656-661). They are accepted by the Sunnis as the rightfully chosen successors of the prophet. On the other hand, the Shi'ites, or Party of 'Ali, opposed the selection of the first three of these caliphs, and since they believed that succession should be hereditary, they believed that 'Ali should have, and in their opinion did succeed the prophet, since he was Muhammad's first cousin and married to Fatima, the prophet's daughter. They believe that on his return from his final pilgrimage, shortly before his death, Muhammad announced that 'Ali was to be his successor. The Sunnis deny this claim.

'Ali was elected the fourth caliph in 656. However, he was immediately attacked by two Companions, Talhah and Zabaya, two of the "Ten Well-betided Ones," who were assured of Paradise by the prophet. They were joined by A'ishah, a widow of the prophet. The three were defeated in battle by 'Ali and his forces. 'Ali also met opposition from Mu'awizah, a relative of the third caliph, 'Uthman, who was governor of Syria. They engaged in a long but inconclusive Battle of Siffon in 647, which in turn led to the secession of the Kharijites, or "Separatists," from 'Ali's army. The Kharijites are an often extremist sect who are fiercely egalitarian and dedicated to divine justice. They wanted Ali to rectify the misdeeds of 'Uthman's administration. 'Ali was able to neutralize most of the Kharijites in a battle. Those who remained set up a rival caliph who never had any power other than within his own community. In fact, 'Ali was assassinated by a Kharijite, Ibn Muljam, in 661. 'Ali's son, Hasan, was elected caliph, but because Mu'awizah threatened to attack him, Hasan gave him the caliphate. When Hasan died his brother Husayn, who was the only other son of 'Ali and Fatima, led a revolt against Mu'awizah in the hope of recovering the caliphate. He was counting on support which had been promised by the men of Kufah but they did not live up to their promise. Husayn and his followers were killed by the forces of Yazid, the Sunni caliph, who was Mu'awizah's son, at Karbala in 680. This was the beginning of a powerful Shi'ite martyrdom tradition.

Husayn's tragic death marks the beginning of Shiism as a religious-political movement. Husayn was gradually seen as a great martyr and Imam, as well as the prototype of God's redemption of the Shi'ites at the end of history. Husayn's death is the central event for Shi'ite Islam. The anniversary of this death, the 10th of Muharran, is the culmination of a turbulent ten-day period of mourning. During this time, some Shi'ites scourge themselves in atonement for their ancestors' abandonment of Husayn to Yazid's army as well as for the perceived betrayal of subsequent Imans, or descendents of 'Ali, who inherited his spiritual mandate. A distinctive religious drama grew up in relation to what had occurred at Karbala. It is a "passion play," as it is known in English, and is known as ta'ziya which means "consolation" in Arabic. It is performed in a variety of ways and with different scripts, in those places were Shi'ites are prominent. Processions accompany the performance. Young men, understood as prototypes of Shi'ites' martyrdom, flagellate themselves with chains and smear their bodies and faces with blood. The fate of 'Ali and his sons is of greatest importance in the Shi'ite scheme of history.

Shi'ite Islam broke into three main divisions because of disagreement over the number of Imams who succeeded Muhammad. It should be noted that in Sunni Islam an Imam is the leader of prayer for a particular occasion or as a regular function. For Shi'ite Islam it is the title for 'Ali and his descendants. They believe that the Imam is religiously inspired, sinless, and the interpreter of God's will as found in Islamic law. But he is not a prophet. The split into three main divisions came, then, as a result of their disagreement over the number of Imams who succeeded Muhammad.

The three groups in question are the Zaydids, who are also called the Fivers, since they recognize five Imams; the Ismailis, also called the Seveners, who recognize seven Imams; and the Ithna Ashari, also called the Twelvers since they accept twelve Imams. The Twelvers are the largest group and are the majority in Iran, Iraq, and Bahrain. The twelfth Imam, Muhammad al-Muntazar (Muhammad, the Awaited One) disappeared as a child in 874, obviously with no sons, which put an end to the line of succession. However, Shi'ite theology teaches that the twelfth Imam did not die but disappeared and is in hiding or "occultation." He will return toward the end of history and will bring about a perfect Muslim society. The Twelve-Imam Shi'ites identify the Mahdi ("the Guided One") with the Twelfth Imam who is called the al-Muntazar ("the Awaited One") as we have seen. The reign of the Mahdi will be followed by the appearance of the Antichrist (ad-Dajjal, literally "the deceiver" or "the imposter") who will appear shortly before Jesus appears at the end of time. According to various hadiths, the Antichrist will seek to lead people into disbelief or to the practice of a false religion. Chaos will result. Then Jesus will return to earth and will destroy the Antichrist and his forces. Jesus, as messiah, will usher in the Day of Judgment. However, the judgment will be made, not by Jesus, but by Allah. Many Sunni Muslims share this world view. However, the identification of the Mahdi with the twelfth Imam is strictly a Shi'ite teaching.

Chapter Three

The Five Pillars of Islam

The five pillars of faith in the Islamic religion are five official acts which are required of all Muslims. They are accepted as such by every branch of the faith. One of the greatest strengths of Islam is its clear theoretical and practical structure. These pillars constitute the common denominator that distinguishes Islam from other religions.

The first pillar, Shahadah ("witnessing") is the most important. Without it, no one can consider himself or herself a Muslim in any sense. It is a confession of faith in one God (Allah) and in God's messenger, Muhammad, and in the teachings of Islam. One testifies: "There is no God but God and Muhammad is the messenger of God." Muslims recognize other messengers including Moses and Jesus. But because they believe much of God's message was distorted or lost, God's full message for humankind was once and for all time revealed to Muhammad. In accepting Muhammad as the "seal of the prophets," Muslims believe that his prophecy corrects and completes all of the previously revealed messages.

The second pillar of faith is salat, which can be translated "prayer" or "worship." What is referred to is mandatory ritual prayer which occurs five times daily: at dawn, noon, midafternoon, just after sunset, and in the evening, between an hour after sunset and mid-night. These prayers are said in the direction of Mecca. Every mosque has a niche called the mihrab which points in the direction of Mecca, which is the birthplace of Islam. It is the place where Abraham worshipped, where Muhammad received the revelation found in the Qur'an, and where Muhammad himself worshipped. Next to the mihrab is the minbar, a raised wooden platform, similar to a pulpit, from which the Imam, the prayer leader, delivers his sermon on Friday, the day of congregational prayer. The service, called ju'mah, is held at mid-day. It is not a day of rest but is a business day. However, it does require a longer break in the routine of one's daily work. Getting time off for Friday prayer is quite difficult for many Muslims in this country.

It is recommended that Muslims observe salat in a mosque but one may pray at home or work or elsewhere as long as the area is clean and free of distractions.

The word "mosque" comes from the arabic "masjid" ("place of prostration") and means a place of worship. Mosques serve a multiplicity of other functions such as a place for personal prayer, theological instruction, and political meetings. Every mosque has one or more Muezzins who make the public call (adhan) to mandatory prayer. In the United States, the adhan is heard publicly in very few places. The adhan includes seven short phrases, namely: God is most great (Allahu Akbar); I bear witness that there is no God but God; I bear witness that Muhammad is God's messenger; Come to prayer; Come to salvation; God is most great; There is no God but God. Most American Muslims have a built-in clock regarding the times of prayer since the public call to prayer is so rare. If it is impossible to observe one of the times of prayer, it can be made up later.

When salat is observed, wudu (ablution) is performed. It is an obligatory cleansing ritual in order to render the believer ritually pure. This is required of both men and women. It consists of washing the hands, mouth, face, arms up to the elbows, and feet. If water is not available, ablutions may be performed by rubbing one's hands through clay or sand and then passing them over one's face and arms.

At prayer, rak'as are performed. A rak'a is a discrete, basic cycle of postures and utterances of which all salats are composed. The word literally means "bowing." When assembled for prayer, the imam, or the prayer leader, begins with, "God is most great," Allahu Akbar. Those present assemble in lines, shoulder to shoulder, and begin to pray: bowing, kneeling, touching the head to the floor, sitting back on their heels, then rising again. Then the worshippers recite the opening sura of the Qur'an with their hands either hanging loosely at their sides or folded in front of their chest. A brief sura or group of verses is recited. Then the phrase, "God is most great" is again recited and the individual bows and says "Glory be to God" and returns to a standing position and again praises God. Then the worshipers prostrate themselves with knees and toes on the floor and the forehead touching the floor with palms flat on the surface on either side of the head. Allahu Akbar is again recited and then a sitting position is taken. Next, a second prostration is carried out, ending with Allahu Akbar and the standing position is resumed. This marks the end of the rak'a. The number of rak'as which are required differs with each of the daily salats: two in the morning, four at noon, afternoon and evening, and three at sunset, seventeen in all. At prayer, females must worship behind men (or in a separate area) since it is regarded as unseemly for a woman to be seen from behind, since the lower part of the body is raised during the prostrations.

Other than the five mandatory daily prayers there are festival prayers, the burial prayer, prayers for rain, prayer at solar and lunar eclipses, and prayer at the beginning of a journey as well as at the return. There is also individual prayer, du'a (literally a "call" or a "plea") which may be spontaneous, with personal petitions, which worship God, thank him, ask for forgiveness, for help, etc. The du'a, whether alone or in a group, is performed with the palms of the hands open to heaven. At the end of this prayer, the words "praise to God" are said and the palms are drawn over the face and then down, crossing over the shoulders. At the end of the salat, the canonical prayer, a du'a normally follows. But a du'a may be made at any time.

The third pillar of the Islamic faith is called "zakat" which means "purification." Muslims are required to give 2.5 percent of their net worth annually for the needy, for propagation of the faith, to free slaves, to relieve debtors, to help travelers, for the administration of zakat, and for the other causes approved by religious authorities. This annual contribution requires 2.5 percent of one's entire wealth and not simply a percentage of one's annual income. Zakat is not really charity since it is based on the belief that human beings are not entitled to ownership but only to stewardship of one's resources. One gives not because he or she is pious but because wealth is not one's own. By means of zakat, a person's wealth is purified for the use of its owner. If zakat is not paid in a given year, then that individual's wealth is considered to be illicitly held and "unclean."

The fourth pillar of Islam is the fast (sawm) during the month of Ramadan (between 28 and 30 days). Ramadan occurs on the ninth month of the Islamic lunar calendar, the month in which the first revelation of the Qur'an came to Muhammad. The lunar calendar loses eleven days every year because it is shorter than the solar calendar. As a results, Ramadan begins approximately eleven days earlier every year and thus, Ramadan can fall in the summer when days are hot and the period from sunrise to sunset is very long.

During Ramadan, Muslims, health permitting, must abstain from dawn to sunset from food, drink, and sexual activity. This fast helps a person to focus on their spiritual life and to identify with those less fortunate. Concessions are made regarding the fast for the old and sick, for pregnant women and those who are breastfeeding, for travelers and those involved in hard manual labor. However, if possible, they are to make up for the days of fasting they have missed.

The fast ends at dusk each evening and a light meal, popularly referred to as break-fast, is eaten. Usually this consists of taking a glass of water and sharing some dates. This ritual of breaking the fast is called iftar and is followed by evening prayers and then by a festive meal. Fasting and sexual continence are practiced during the day, but according to a revelation he received, Muhammad abrogated the prohibition against sexual intercourse on the nights of Ramadan (Sura 2:187). During Ramadan, many Muslims read the entire Qur'an. Yet Ramadan is not a somber period. At night, friends and family not only gather to eat and pray, but also to enjoy one another's company. During the last ten days of Ramadan, on one of which nights the Qur'an was first revealed, a celebration of the "Night of Power" is observed. It is the holiest night in the Islamic calendar year. No one knows with certainty which night the prophet received the first revelation but it is odd-numbered. Most believe it is the twenty-seventh night. Nevertheless, all observe the "Night of Power" in thanksgiving for the revelation of the Qur'an. The month of Ramadan ends with one of the two major Islamic feasts, the Feast of the Breaking of the Fast, called 'Eid al Fitr. In Muslim-majority areas, businesses are closed and everywhere invitations are extended to family, friends, and neighbors to join the celebration. Children are given gifts and all enjoy the festivities.

The fifth pillar is the pilgrimage to Mecca, called the Hajj. Every adult is required to undertake this pilgrimage, if possible, once during his or her lifetime, though most cannot afford to do so. Often a family or a whole village saves so that at least one of them can make the hajj, to the blessing of all.

Mecca is a forbidden city to non-Muslims because of its holiness. This includes a minimum radius of five kilometers, slightly more than three miles, from the Ka'ba in all directions. Medina is also open only to Muslims but a visit to the tomb of the prophet is not mandatory for Muslims. A visit to the tomb of the prophet, which is in Medina, is made by many pilgrims.

The pilgrimage takes place during the month of Dhu al-Hijja, not long after the month of Ramadan. More than two million of the faithful make the hajj every year. Male pilgrims wear two seamless white cloths which symbolize purity as well as the unity and equality of all believers. Women wear clothing that entirely covers their body except for their face and hands. Pilgrims enter Mecca through a number of checkpoints and as they approach Mecca, they shout, "I am here, O Lord. I am here." They put themselves into a state of purity known as Ihram, which includes the wearing of the white seamless garments. It is a special state of purity necessary to perform the pilgrimage. Certain things are forbidden: sexual intercourse, clipping the nails, hunting, wearing perfume or jewelry, cutting the hair, uprooting living things, arguing, and talking about the opposite sex. Men are required to keep their heads uncovered and women must keep their heads covered.

The pilgrimage involves a series of sometimes strenuous and complicated rituals, usually performed with the help of a pilgrim guide. When they enter Mecca, their first obligation is to go to the Ka'ba which is located within the compound of the Grand Mosque. The pilgrims walk counterclockwise around the Ka'ba seven times, which symbolizes their entry into God's presence. As the hajj continues, they next walk and sometimes run along a quarter-mile corridor of the Grand Mosque seven times to commemorate Hagar's frantic search in the desert for water for herself and her son Ishmael. This ritual symbolizes humankind's ongoing persistence in life's struggle for survival. The pilgrims drink water from a well called Zamzan ("bubbling") which is located within the Grand Mosque. This is the well where Muslims believe God provided water for Hagar and Ishmael. Next, the pilgrims assemble for a day on the plain of Arafat in commemoration of Muhammad's final pilgrimage. It was here, from the Mount of Mercy, a hill in the middle of the plain, that the prophet delivered his farewell sermon. At the next station in the pilgrimage they symbolically reject the devil by throwing stones at three pillars which are located at the site where Satan met Abraham and Ishmael, and tempted Abraham to disobey God when he was preparing to sacrifice Ishmael in obedience to God's command.

The final ritual takes place when the pilgrims sacrifice animals in commemoration of Abraham's sacrifice of a ram which was provided by God in place of Ishmael after Abraham's faith had been tested. This event, which is celebrated by Muslims everywhere, is known as the Feast of Sacrifice, or 'Eid al Adha. This is the greater of the two canonical Muslim feasts celebrated each year, the other being 'Eid al Fitr, the Breaking of the Fast, at the close of Ramadan. 'Eid al Adha is celebrated worldwide for three days and is a time of rejoicing and sharing. Whoever sacrifices an animal, for example, sheep, goats, cows, or camels, must share a third with needy persons, a third with neighbors, and the final third with his own family.

Chapter Four

Sufism

The word "Sufism" is derived from the Arabic word "suf" (wool) and refers to the coarse woolen garments worn by the first sufis. Whereas shari'ah (law) provides the rights and duties of the individual and the community, Sufism is the path of mysticism. Just as in other mystical movements in Christianity, Judaism, Hinduism, and Buddhism, the sufis follow a way of purification, a discipline of mind and body, whose goal is to directly experience God. Its doctrines and methods are derived from the Qur'an and Islamic revelation. Despite any borrowings and influences from exterior sources, the essence of Sufism is purely Islamic. Contrary to some popular religious notions found in the West, to embark upon the path of Sufism, it is absolutely necessary to be a Muslim. Sufism's methods are basically inoperative without this religious affiliation.

Sufism began as a reform movement as a response to the materialism of Muslim society as it developed even greater power and wealth. Sufis seek to find God not in wealth and power but in an effort to practice self-denial as they strive for personal unity with God. Sufis work in the world in contrast to Christian monasticism and its tradition of withdrawing from the world in order to find God. There is neither monastery nor monasticism in Islam. Sufis are married men, often with large families, who work in a great variety of professions. Women have not attained equal rights, even in Sufism. Female Sufis have to lead their own religious lives or join one of the existing male orders, and if they do they have a clearly inferior status. Even as mystical disciples, they have to maintain a certain distance from men. This is achieved during services by the use of veils or curtains which separate the sexes.

Sufis found the emphasis on laws, duties, and rules to be lacking spiritually. Instead, they sought to follow an interior path and to fulfill God's will by means of prayer, fasting, and meditating on the Qur'an, making God the center of their lives, avoiding the desire for material possessions, and performing good works. The original Sufis were not mystics in the real sense of proclaiming a doctrine of experience and unity with God. For example, Al-Hasan al-Basri (643-728), who later mystics as well as theologians claimed as their ancestor, was not a mystic who strove to be one with God. Rather, he was an ascetic who simply wanted to live a life pleasing to God in the midst of the world. The emphasis on renunciation of the world and meditation was complemented by the teaching of Rabia al-Adawiyya (d. 801) who fused asceticism with deep devotional love of God. This joining of the ascetic with the ecstatic permanently influenced the nature and development of Sufism. It transformed Sufism from a movement which had a rather elite following to one that appealed to every strata of society. Throughout the ninth and tenth centuries, Sufism grew in Arabia, Syria, Iraq, and Egypt.

As Sufism became a mass movement, the religious leaders, the ulama, felt the sufis had gone too far since they felt the supremacy of shari'ah (Islamic Law) and their own prerogatives and authority were being challenged. However, despite the continued differences between the two groups, the writing of Abu Hamid al-Ghazali (1058-1111) secured a place for Sufism within the Muslim community. Al-Ghazali was well versed in theology, law, and philosophy and for many years he studied and practiced Sufism. His great work, *The Revivication of the Religious Sciences*, is a synthesis of law, theology, and mysticism. He presented law and theology in a way acceptable to the ulama but these disciplines, as he described them, were grounded in direct religious experience.

The twelfth century witnessed not only the legitimation of Sufism by al-Ghazali but also the formation of the first great Sufi orders. And as John Esposito observes:

> By the thirteenth century, Sufism began to be transformed from loose, voluntary associations into organized brotherhoods or religious orders (tariqahs) of mendicants...with their own distinctive institutions.

He goes on to say:

> By the thirteenth century, Sufi orders had created international networks of centers that transformed Sufism into a popular mass movement whose preachers were the great missionaries of Islam.

Sufi centers were founded everywhere, and as Hans Kung observes in *Islam: Past, Present and Future*, ". . . institutional and doctrinal limits were instituted within Sufism to consolidate the thousands of Sufi communities spiritually and regulate them at least minimally."[2] Kung notes that in the twelfth and thirteenth centuries, the Sufi networks "took on the features of religious orders – despite essential differences they were not unlike the Christian religious orders which were developing at the same time in Europe."[3] Kung points out that in the Christian religious orders, and among the Sufis, the following ideals were found, namely love of God and service to one's neighbor, subordination to superiors, a distinctive rule, a distinctive mode of dress, a special type of prayers, and so on.

The Sufis continued to be viewed with suspicion and hostility by the ulama who feared that the gathering places of the brotherhoods would supplant the mosque and that Sufism would challenge the supremacy of shari'ah (Islamic Law) as the key to carrying out God's will on earth. The brotherhoods, formed around holy places and tombs of the "saints," used poetic expression that avoided direct challenges to orthodoxy, and they flourished because they filled a spiritual need among the faithful.

The goal of the Sufi was a direct knowledge or personal religious experience of God's presence. In order to achieve this, Sufis believe one must die to the ego-centered self. The path that must be followed involves three states: renunciation, purification, and insight or knowledge. Here, knowledge is not mere mental knowledge but identity between the knower and the one known (God). Many practices are adopted to help one attain this goal, such as voluntary poverty, maintaining periods of silence, fasting, and other disciplines. Remembrance (dhikr) of God's name through rhythmic, repetitive invocations of His name(s) is done many, many times daily to focus on God's immediate presence. Another approach (dhikr) is the recitation of a litany of God's names or attributes, often with the use of a string of prayer beads similar to a rosary. The idea is that when a person is involved in such recitations, he or she forgets about worldly desires and becomes even closer to God. Yet another form of dhikr is the use of music, dance, and concerts of devotional poems to induce ecstatic states in which the believers might experience the presence of God or union with God. The best known use of the dance is that of the Whirling Dervishes who are members of the order founded by Jalal al-Din Rumi (1207-1273), who was one of the greatest mystics of Islam.

Rumi was of Persian origin, born in Balkr, now in northern Afghanistan. His father was a distinguished theologian who had an interest in Sufism. His influence on his son was notable. To avoid the Mongol invasion of their country, his family traveled through Persia and other Near Eastern countries and for a time settled in Mecca. On their return, they settled in Iconium, now Konya, Turkey. Because of the Byzantine past of the region, it retained the name Rum ("Rome") among the Turks. It is from this that Jalal al-Din came to be known as ar-Rumi, "the man of Rome (Byzantium)."

In Konya, Rumi met with important spiritual guides who had come to reside in that city. The most important of these was Shams al-Din al Tabrizi, who arrived in 1244. Shams, considered to be one of the greatest spiritual teachers of the time, had great influence on Rumi and led him to a deep desire for the direct knowledge of God. *The Mathnawi*, a vast, six-volume work of spiritual teaching and Sufi lore in the form of stories and lyric poetry, stands as one of the treasures of the Persian-speaking world. In this work, written between 1247 and his death in 1273, Rumi composed thousands of rhymed couplets. They were collected into *The Mathnawi*, 25,000 couplets in all.

Rumi founded the Mevlevi order of Sufis known as the Whirling Dervishes for their dancing and music, both of which are supports for their spiritual method. Apart from the dancing and music of the Dervishes, Rumi is associated with music in another way, since the singing of the poetry of *The Mathnawi* has become an art form in itself.

To this day, Rumi's tomb in Konya is a place of pilgrimage for many Muslims and others. One of the most famous quotations from Rumi is a sign of his direct mystical experience with God. He wrote:

Tell me Muslims, what should be done?
  I don't know how to defend myself. I am neither Christian nor Jewish, neither pagan nor Muslim.
  I don't hail from the East or from the West.
  I am neither for land nor sea.
  I am not a creature of the world.
  Criticism is as old as Sufism itself. As John Esposito observes:
  The very characteristics that accounted for the strength of Sufism and its effectiveness and success as a popular religious force, contributed to its degeneration. The same flexibility, tolerance, and eclecticism that had enabled Sufism to spread and incorporate local customs and practices from Africa to Southeast Asia and attract many converts permitted the most bizarre and antinomian practices to enter and run wild.[4]

Beginning in the twelfth and thirteenth centuries and continuing to the end of the eighteenth century, a veneration of saints and cults at the tombs of saints became the main vehicle of Sufi Islam. In fact, during these centuries, the veneration of shrines and holy places became the most widespread form of Islamic religious life. Sufi leaders provided spiritual counsel, medical cures, and mediations between different groups who were in need of settling their disputes. As Hans Kung notes of these Sufi leaders:

They taught children and healed the sick, distributed amulets, practiced white magic and functioned as mediators between the human world of human beings and the world of spirits and the divine. This was a dilution of the religious substance of Islam and a change of focus that inevitably provoked criticism.[5]

Sufism often became anti-intellectual and some of its leaders mocked the founders of the great schools of Islamic law and attacked philosophers, including Ibn Sina (Avicenna) who was also a mystic.

Criticism of Sufi veneration of saints, the cult of tombs, the divinization of sheikhs, and self-divinization came from many quarters in different Islamic countries. Conservatives called for a return to the original Islam but often to no avail. In the eighteenth and nineteenth centuries, the Wahhabi movement in Arabia abolished Sufism. In Turkey in 1925, the head of the new secular government in that country, Mustafa Kemal (Attaturk) banned the politically reactionary order of the Whirling Dervishes. That is no longer the case today.

Today, many of the excesses no longer exist and Sufism is still practiced by many Muslims since it meets their religious needs. Instead of concentrating on doctrine, Sufism allows for the expression of religious feelings in music, dance, and festivals. Still, many intellectuals and politicians see Sufism as an outdated tradition which needs to be discarded.

NOTES

1. John L. Esposito, *Islam: The Straight Path* (New York: Oxford University Press, 1998), 108.

2. Hans Kung, *Islam: Past, Present and Future* (New York: One World Publication, English translation, 2007), 336.

3. *Ibid.*, 337.

4. Esposito, *Islam: The Straight Path, op. cit.*, 112.

5. Kung, *op. cit.*, 112.

Part II

CURRENT AREAS OF CONCERN

Chapter Five

The Role of Women in Islam

An issue which has unfavorably influenced the non-Islamic world is that of the status of women in Islam. It is important to realize there is much more to the Islamic view of women than polygamy or the wearing of the burqa, i.e., the full covering of a woman which leaves only the eyes visible, or the chador, an Iranian term for the covering of the hair and body, leaving only the face, hands, and feet exposed. The rules governing the status and conduct of women in Muslim countries have their origin as deeply in local and tribal conditions as they do in official Islamic teaching. For this reason, it is very difficult to generalize about the status of women in Islam. What is true of women in one country is not true of those in another country. The differences are based more on local custom, education, and economics than on religious doctrine.

It is interesting to note that many of the rights that modern women in Western society now take for granted, after having fought and struggled to obtain them in the latter part of the nineteenth and well into the middle of the twentieth century, have been basic under Islamic Law for Muslim women for over fourteen centuries—even though these rights have often been ignored. Among these are:

1. The right to own property, business(es), buy/sell/trade, enter into contracts/leases/purchases, without interference of husband, father, brother, or any other male.
2. The right to inherit, keep it, and to do what she wants with it, without interference of her husband, father, brother, or any other male. Meanwhile, her husband has to provide her food, clothing, and shelter from his own income, labor, or inheritance without her having to contribute anything.

3. The woman's rights in marriage include:
    a. The right to choose her husband (and the right of refusal);
    b. The right to a dowry which is hers to keep and is not available to her husband, father, or guardian;
    c. The right to a pre-nuptial agreement, the violation of which is grounds for divorce;
    d. The right to be cared for by her husband: fed, clothed and given shelter, the violation of which can be grounds for divorce;
    e. The right to be treated kindly and fairly;
    f. The right to divorce if abandoned, abused, or maltreated by her husband;
    g. Conjugal rights;
    h. The right to vote and participate in the affairs of the Muslim community;
    i. The right to an education.

It is also clear, based on the Qur'an and the Sunnah (Tradition), that the woman is equal to man in the eyes of God. Traditionalists stress that while men and women are indeed equal before God, they have complementary, not identical, roles in society. That being said, it would be disingenuous to claim that the Qur'an grants women an equal place in society. As is true of traditional Judaism and Christianity, Islam is a basically a patriarchal religion. Leadership of the community belongs to man. The Qur'an takes for granted that men lead the community. They fight, hunt, preach, and make laws. The role of women is to raise children and tend to domestic duties. This function remains true today but many Islamic women are now well educated and play prominent roles in the medical field, education, the political arena, and in other important areas.

Many of these educated women are now quite active in participating in observances in the mosque. In the past, it was more common for women to pray at home. This was due to the restriction of women in their home and their limited education. Some did attend the Friday congregational prayer though rather few in number and separated from the men.

A great many of the changes brought about by education, it must be pointed out, have impacted a rather small proportion of Islamic women and the number varies from one country to another and even within various regions of the same country. Concerning this issue, John L. Esposito writes:

> Today, in many Muslim countries, particularly those that have been regarded as among the most modernized, such as Egypt, Tunisia, Jordan and Malaysia, women are forming their own prayer and Qur'an study groups, which, in some cases, are led by women imams. They cite the example of Muslim women who

were reputed for their knowledge and sanctity as justification for their present activities.[1]

In Islam, marriage is accomplished by a contract. Normally, marriages are not contracted in mosques but in private homes before an imam or in the office of a judge. When agreement to the marriage is expressed and witnessed, those present recite the fatihah (the opening sura of the Qur'an). It is often the national or tribal customs which determine the type of ceremony and the celebration which accompanies it. For example, in some parts of the Islamic world, receptions are held where the bride is adorned in elaborate jewelry, or the bride might be carried in a litter to her new home.

Religious law permits a Muslim male to marry a Jewish or Christian woman, or a Sabian (a monotheist of some other religion). However, it is forbidden for a Muslim woman to marry a non-Muslim.

Divorce is allowed, even though a statement attributed to Muhammad maintains: "Of all things licit, the most hateful to God is divorce." Historically, women have had little right to seek a divorce, but a man could do so easily without having to provide any justification for doing so. This right of males is not found in the Qur'an which guarantees equality to women in this matter. Sura 2:228 states: "And women have rights equal to what is incumbent upon them to what is just". The quality of rights includes the right of a woman to divorce her husband and this right is reflected in hadith literature. Legal reformers cite the Qur'an and hadiths to support contemporary reforms in divorce laws.

In fact, Islam does not encourage divorce nor permit it to be undertaken lightly. Marriage in Islam can be terminated (a) by repudiation of the husband; (b) by mutual consent; (c) by judicial dissolution by the court upon the request of the wife.

In repudiation, the husband says to the wife, "I divorce you." He must say this three times. It is legally possible to state these three repudiations at one time but it is considered morally reprehensible to do so. The repudiation must be delivered while the wife is in a state of purity, that is, not menstruating, and the husband must not have relations with her during this period. Also, the woman must not be pregnant. The repudiation must be followed by a period of waiting for three menstrual periods to determine if there is a pregnancy and implicitly to facilitate reconciliation. If the wife is pregnant, the divorce cannot take place until the allotted time after the birth of the child. During the "'iddah" (the duration of the menstrual periods), the husband must supply his wife with upkeep, lodging, and food. An allowance beyond these necessities is morally, but not legally, required.

The divorce is immediately revocable by the husband at any time during the 'iddah. However, if the statement of divorce is repeated in each of the ensuing months for a total of three repudiations, reconciliation becomes very difficult. In fact, afterwards, remarriage is required but this cannot occur unless the woman subsequently remarries and is then divorced from her second husband. It seems clear that to view Islam as permitting an easy divorce on the part of the husband is misleading. The cumulative effect of the above regulations is to restrict what previously had been a casual practice.

In the West, polygamy is usually regarded as typically Islamic, though it was widespread in the ancient Near East. In these warrior societies, polygamy probably also had the purpose of providing for the widows of warriors. The number of widows brought about by war was usually high. The Qur'an permits a man to have four wives. Sura 4:3 states "Marry such women as seem good to you two, three, four; but if you fear you will not be not equitable, then only one." Islamic law mandates that if there is more than one wife, each is to be treated equally in terms of support and affection. This includes separate housing (depending on finances, a room, an apartment, or a house) and maintenance. A corollary verse, 4:129, states "You are never able to be fair and just between women even if that is your ardent desire." This verse has been used by some contemporary reformers in the Muslim community to reject the possibility of equal justice among wives. They therefore argue that the Quranic ideal is monogamy. Others disagree with this argument. This much is clear: the law is equivocal on the subject of polygamy. The Qur'an permits polygamy, but in terms that limit the practice. Polygamy is practiced by a very small number of Muslims. It is by no means the norm and some Islamic countries have simply outlawed plural marriage altogether, and severe limitations have been placed on it in other countries.

In 2007, John L. Esposito and Dalia Magahed wrote *Who Speaks for Islam: What a Billion Muslims Really Think.* This work is based on the Gallup Global Poll which is an ongoing survey of respondents in more than 130 countries and areas, and its results are representative of 95% of the world's population. The Gallup Poll of the Muslim World, the basis of the findings presented in this book, is part of this initiative. As stated in Appendix B:

> The Gallup World Poll is a self-funded study conducted purely for research—not advocacy—purposes. Gallup has never done polling for any political party or advocacy group, and it never will. The purity and objectivity of the data and analysis are the foundation of Gallup's business model and the core of its brand.[2]

Dr. Esposito is a professor of religion and international affairs and of Islamic studies at Georgetown University, and the founding director of Georgetown's Prince Alwaleed Bin Talal Center for Muslim-Christian Understanding. He is the past president of the American Council for the study of Islamic

Societies. His more than 35 books include *What Everybody Needs to Know About Islam and Unholy War: Terrorism in the Name of Islam.*

Dalia Magahed is the senior analyst of Gallup's unprecedented study of more than one billion Muslims worldwide. She also directs the Muslim-West Facts Initiative through which Gallup, in collaboration with the Coexist Foundation, is disseminating the findings of the Gallup World Poll to key opinion leaders in the Muslim world and the West. Her analysis has appeared in a number of leading publications including *The Economist*, *The Wall Street Journal, Harvard International Review*, and many other academic and popular journals.

The book written by Esposito and Magahed is the product of a mammoth multi-year Gallup research study as has been mentioned. As they observe:

> Between 2001 and 2007, Gallup conducted tens of thousands of hour-long, face-to-face interviews with the residents of more than 35 nations that are predominantly Muslim or have substantial Muslim populations. The sample represents young and old, educated and illiterate, female and male, and from urban and rural settings. With the random sampling method that Gallup used, results are valid within a plus or minus 3-point margin of error. In totality, we surveyed a sample representing more than 90% of the world's 1.3 billion Muslims, making this the largest, most comprehensive study of contemporary Muslims ever done.[3]

The authors go on to state:

> Gallup's research produced a number of insights, but the most important was this: The conflict between the Muslim and Western communities is far from inevitable. It is more about policy than principles. However, until and unless decision makers listen directly to the people and gain an accurate understanding of this conflict, extremists on all sides will continue to gain ground.[4]

Who Speaks For Islam? is composed of five chapters, namely, Who are Muslims? Democracy or Theocracy? What Makes a Radical? What Do Women Want? And Clash or Coexistence? Insights from these chapters and the data they represent will be used when relevant in the remaining chapters of this book.

The remainder of this chapter will focus on the data concerning women found in the chapter, What Do Women Want? The results of the Gallup survey are enlightening and in many respects, surprising.

In sharp contrast to the Western perception of the repressive lives Islamic women lead, the Gallup findings of women in predominantly Muslim countries or nations that have large Muslim populations present an entirely different view. The majority of the women surveyed believe that women deserve the same legal rights as men, including the right to vote without any interference from family members; the right to work at any job they are qualified for; and the right to participate and serve in government, including the highest levels. Even in Saudi Arabia, the results of the poll remain constant. As Esposito and Magahed state:

> In Saudi Arabia, for example, where as of this writing, women were not allowed to vote or drive, majorities of women say that women should be able to drive a car by themselves (61%), vote without influence (69%), and work at any job for which they are qualified (76%).[5]

It is interesting that in Saudi Arabia, only 8% of the men say they believe women should have the right to vote.

In regard to education, naturally representative, self-reported data show percentages of women in Iran (52%), Egypt (34%), Saudi Arabia (32%), and Lebanon (37%) have post-secondary education. In the United Arab Emirates and Iran, women outnumber men at the university level. However, this is not the case in other countries. Gallup found a wide range of female education. Percentages of women pursuing post-secondary education were only 8% in Morocco and 13% in Pakistan. In Yemen, women's literacy is only 28% versus 70% for men; in Pakistan it is 28% versus 53% for men. On the other hand, women's literacy in Iran and Saudi Arabia is 70%, and 85% in Jordan and Malaysia. The UNESCO 2005 Gender and Development report states that the ratio of women to men enrolled in secondary education in 2001-2002 was equal or higher than male enrollment in Jordan, Algeria, Lebanon, Kuwait, Libya, the United Arab Emirates, Indonesia, Malaysia, and Bangladesh. In many Muslim countries, it is clear that in regard to the education of women, the repressive attitude of the Taliban in Afghanistan in the 1990s does not exist.

The Gallup data concerning Muslim women and their attitudes toward the West are complex. The majority of Muslim women admire much about the West but do not yearn to become more like their Western counterparts. While they favor gender equality, they want it on their own terms and within their own cultural context. This includes their mode of dress. Among the most admired aspects of the West, high percentages of women and men cite political freedom, free speech, and gender equality. But in response to the statement "adopting Western values will help in their progress," very few accepted this notion. For example, only 12% of Indonesian women, 20% of Iranian women, and 18% of Turkish women, who are usually assumed to be the most favorable towards Westernization, accept this statement as applying to them. The Pew Global Attitudes Project in 2006 reported that in the Middle East and Asia, majorities of Muslims in Egypt, Jordan, and Pakistan do not believe that women are respected in Western societies.[6] The data do not support the popular Western perception that Islamic women want to be liberated from their culture and adopt Western values.

In regard to their faith, substantial majorities of Muslim women in virtually all predominantly or substantially Muslim countries surveyed by Gallup say that their religion is an important part of their life. They also believe that Islam is their society's greatest asset. Muslim women do not regard Islam as an obstacle to their progress but rather see it as a critical component of that progress. Asifa Quraish, a law professor at the University of Wisconsin and an advocate of women's rights, argues "that the most effective means to oppose practices done in the name of Shariah that are hurtful to women is to challenge the compliance of these laws to Islamic principles, instead of arguing for the removal of Shariah." In regard to the attitude of Western feminists, Qurashi argues that Western feminists often have basic misconceptions about Islam and Islamic law and sometimes have an "innate, often subconscious sense of superiority" and approach issues facing Muslim women with a "rescue mentality."[7]

There are certainly gender gaps in the Muslim world, with men holding the upper hand in many countries. However, the Gallup surveys show that gender equality is not mentioned at all in Jordan and mentioned by only 1% of women in Egypt and 2% in Morocco. It is mentioned by 5% of women in Saudi Arabia. Muslim women, like Muslim men, say that their most pressing issues include, primarily, economic development and political reform. The need for political reform includes the issue of women's rights since democracy is strongly favored, again within their own cultural framework, and there can be no real democracy in the Muslim world that does not recognize and include women as full and equal participants in all spheres of life. It is also clear that economic development is necessary and the role of women in helping to bring this about is of great importance.

NOTES

1. Esposito, *Islam: The Straight Path*, *op. cit.*, 190.
2. Esposito and Magahed, *Who Speaks For Islam?*, *op. cit.*, 175.
3. *Ibid.*, x, xi.
4. *Ibid.*, xi.
5. *Ibid.*, 102.
6. Retrieved September 18, 2007, from http://oew.global.org/reports/display pap? Report ID=253.
7. *Ibid.*, 119.

Chapter Six

The Islamic Jesus

Jesus holds an exalted place in Islam. The Qur'an says that Jesus was born of the Virgin Mary (3:45-47). He is called the "spirit of God" because Mary conceived him through the action of the spirit. He is also called "word of God." This does not mean a preexistent divine being or a divine person. Rather, it refers to the creative word of God which Jesus as God's messenger points to. The announcement of the birth of Jesus and his virginal conception is narrated at length twice—in Surah's 19:16-22 and 3:42-47. Surah 19:16-22 states:

Relate in the Book
(The story of) Mary,
When she withdrew
From her family
To a place in the East.

She placed a screen
(to screen herself) from them;
Then we sent to her
Our angel, and he appeared
Before her as a man
In all respects.

She said: "I seek refuge
From thee to (Allah)
Most gracious (come not near)
If thou dost fear Allah.

He said, "Nay I am only
A messenger from thy Lord,

(To announce to the
The gift of a holy son."

She said: "How shall I
Have a son, seeing that
No man has touched me,
And I am not unchaste?"

He said: "So (it will be):
The Lord saith, That is
Easy for me – and (We)
Wish to appoint him
As a sign unto men
And a mercy from us:
It is a matter
(So decreed).

So she conceived him.
And she retired with him
To a remote place.[1]

In the Qur'an, Jesus is usually referred to as "son of Mary." His titles include Messiah, Prophet, Messenger of God, and "one of those brought nigh (to God). According to various hadith as messenger Jesus will return before the Day of Judgment and destroy the Anti-Christ who, towards the end of time, will present an inverted vision of spirituality, misleading humankind. The Qur'an speaks of Jesus appearing at the Last Judgment but not as a judge but as a "witness," who bears witness to God for the Christians.

In the Qur'an, Jesus is a prophet and messenger of God of the highest order, in the same line as Adam, Noah, David, Solomon, and Moses, who preached the same message, that there is only one God. However, the Qur'an rejects the claim that Jesus is divine, the Son of God. This idea is seen as a mistaken interpretation by Jesus' followers. The New Testament title that is most important for Christian dogma, "Son of God," does not appear in the Qur'an. Muslims see this title as an insult to the transcendence of God.

According to the Qur'an, Jesus worked miracles including healing the sick and raising the dead. He worked these miracles with God's permission and power. Great as he is, Jesus is a human being, not divine. He is a servant of God.

The Qur'an teaches that Jesus did not die on the cross. Surah 4:15 states: "That they said (in boast), 'We killed Christ Jesus, the son of Mary, the messenger of Allah' – but they killed him not, nor crucified him, but so it was made to appear to them, and those who differ therein are full of doubts, with no certain knowledge, but only conjecture to follow, for a surety they killed him not." It is the common belief among Muslims that the crucifixion was an illusion or, more commonly, that someone else was substituted for Jesus. In fact, the crucifixion of Jesus does not play a role in Islamic teaching any more than does the question of his divine nature. Salvation in Islam is based on God's oneness and the fact that God is absolute. One's life is judged on his or her obedience to God and not on redemption brought about by Jesus' sacrifice as is taught in Christianity. Surah 4:158 states, "Nay, Allah raised him up unto Himself; and Allah is exalted in power, Wise." In his commentary on this verse, Abdullah Yusuf 'Ali writes:

> There is a different opinion as to the exact interpretation of this verse. The words are: The Jews did not kill Jesus, but Allah raised him up (ra-fa'a) to Himself. One school holds that Jesus did not die the usual human death, but still lives in the body in heaven, which is the generally accepted Muslim view. Another holds that he did die but not when he was supposed to be crucified, and that his being "raised up" unto Allah means that instead of being disgraced as a malefactor, as the Jews intended, he was on the contrary honoured by Allah as his messenger. . . ."[2]

The generally accepted interpretation, that Jesus did not die and will return at the end of time does not, as in Christian belief, involve a resurrection which is central to the Christian faith. And from what has been said, it should be clear that Islam does not accept the idea of the Trinity. The crucial teaching of Islam is the oneness of God (Tawhid). Tawhid is the defining doctrine of Islam. It declares an absolute monotheism – the unity and uniqueness of God as creator and sustainer of the universe. Surah 4:171 states:

> O People of the Book! Commit no excesses in your religion: nor say of Allah ought but the truth. Christ Jesus the son of Mary was (no more than) a messenger of Allah and His word, which he bestowed on Mary and a Spirit proceeding from Him: so believe in Allah and his messengers. Say not "Trinity": desist: it will be better for you: for Allah is one God: glory be to him: (Far exalted is He) above having a son. . . ."[3]

Tawhid is at the forefront of Islamic thought today due to a concern with the practical manifestations of Islamic unity in a world fragmented by colonialism and nationalism. Tawhid has emerged as a powerful symbol of divine, spiritual, and sociopolitical unity.

As mother of Jesus, Mary has a special place in the Qur'an and therefore in popular Muslim piety. She is the only woman mentioned by name in the Islamic scriptures. An entire chapter is devoted to Mary, who is mentioned more often in the Qur'an than in the New Testament. Concerning Mary, the

Qur'an includes: the pregnancy of her mother, Anna, the birth of Mary, the annunciation of the birth of John the Baptist and of Jesus, her virginal conception and the birth of Jesus. The Qur'an teaches that Mary is to be revered since she submitted herself to God's will in regard to the virgin birth, even though her own family would accuse her of unchastity when it discovered that she was pregnant (19:16-21). The Qur'an also teaches that Jesus, as an infant, verbally defended his mother's innocence (19:27-34). The title "Mother of God" is never used and, in fact, is obviously rejected. It may be because of this title that there is a misunderstanding of the Christian Trinity in the Qur'an. Surah 5:116 implies that Mary is the second person of the Trinity. Allah is the first person and Jesus, the Son, is the third person. It is clear that the Qur'an teaches that there is only one God, without partners or descendents (Tahwid). Joseph, the husband of Mary in the Gospels, is not mentioned in the Qur'an.

When the Muslims conquered Mecca in 630, the Ka'ba was cleansed of the many stone and wooden idols it contained. Inside the Ka'ba, on one of the walls, were several paintings as well as an icon of the Virgin and Child. Out of respect for Jesus and Mary, Muhammad covered the icon with his hands, indicating it should be preserved, instructing that everything else should be covered over.

NOTES

1. 'Abdullah Yusuf 'Ali, *The Holy Quran, op. cit.*, 747-748.
2. *Ibid.*
3. *Ibid.*, 239-240.

Chapter Seven

The Muslim Gospel

The Arabic Islamic literary tradition of the pre-modern period contains several hundred sayings and stories ascribed to Jesus. Tarif Khalidi, in his book *The Muslim Jesus*, presents a collection of these sayings and stories.[1] Dr. Khalidi is Shaykr Zazid bin Sultan Professor of Arabic and Islamic Studies at the Center for Arab and Middle Eastern Studies at the American University of Beirut, Lebanon. Formerly he was Sir Thomas Adam's Professor of Arabic, Director of the Center of Middle Eastern and Islamic Studies, and Fellow of King's College, Cambridge, England. He is the author of numerous books. Dr. Khalidi observes that, as a whole, the collection forms the largest body of texts relating to Jesus in any non-Christian literature. Khalidi refers to this body of literature as the "Muslim Gospel." His purpose is to introduce an image of Jesus little known outside the Arabic Islamic culture. This literature shows how Jesus was perceived by a religious tradition which greatly revered him but rejected his divinity. Khalidi writes:

> The Muslim gospel is not found as a complete corpus in any one Arabic Islamic source. Rather, it is scattered in works of ethics and popular devotion, works of Adab (belles-lettres), works of Sufism or Muslim mysticism, anthologies of wisdom and histories of prophets and saints. The sources range in time from the second/eighth century to the twelfth/eighteenth century. [Khalidi notes that in such time expressions the number preceding the slash indicates the Islamic date, A.H., or anno hegirae; the one following the slash notes the Christian date, A.D., or anno domini.] As regards the sayings and stories, these vary in size from a single sentence to a story of several hundred words. They circulated in Arabic Islamic literature and lore all the way from Spain to China, and some of them remain familiar to educated Muslims today.[2]

Khalidi stresses that Jesus does not appear alone in Islamic works of piety and asceticism. He is found in a genre of religious literature called "Tales of the Prophets." He is accompanied by other Qur'anic prophets to whom sayings and stories were also ascribed. Prominent among these prophets are Moses, David, Solomon, Job, Luqman, and John the Baptist. Luqman is a figure mentioned in the Qur'an in Surah 31:11 as "a man having wisdom." He was known in Arab legend as a sage, and later tradition attached to his name a corpus of proverbs and moral tales. Khalidi points out that amid this literature as a whole, Jesus stands out for the quantity and above all the quality of his sayings and stories. He writes, "Whereas the sayings and tales of other prophets tend to conform to specific and narrowly defined moral types, the range and continuous growth of the Jesus corpus had not parallels among other prophets in the Muslim tradition."[3]

These sayings and stories have their origin in Hadith, a word which has a fairly wide range of meanings: a report, an account, a tale, a tradition related by a Companion of the Prophet, from some highly regarded spiritual figure of the early days of Islamic history, considered to be a spiritual Successor (Tabi'i) of the Companions, and from ancient revealed scriptures or religious lore of the Judaic and Christian traditions.

The Qur'an was concerned with rectifying the Christian doctrinal image of Jesus as divine and had little to say on his ministry and teachings. The Muslim gospel probably arose from a felt need to complement and expand the Qur'anic account of his life. Concerning this, Khalidi writes: "In this limited respect, the process of formation of the Muslim gospel can be compared to the formation of the apocryphal and other extracanonical materials in the Christian tradition, and probably for the same reasons."[4]

The city of Kufa in Iraq was in all likelihood the original home of the Muslim gospel, although other cities and regions such as Basra, Mecca, Medina, Syria, and Egypt were also represented by important transmitters of these hadith. Kufa has long been recognized for its seminal importance in the genesis of systematic Islamic scholarship so the fact that it was the original home of the Muslim gospel is not surprising. Kufa scholars are regularly found at the origin of religious subjects such as Hadith, Qur'anic exegesis, theology, and jurisprudence.

Al Ghazali's (d. 505/1111) *The Revival of Religious Sciences* contains the largest number of sayings attributed to Jesus in any Islamic text. In the strictly ethical sections of this very influential book, Khalidi tells us:

> . . . that a full understanding of the mysteries of the heart and its innermost nature is beyond the reach of the human intellect. Hence the need for metaphors and parables (anthal) to express these mysteries; and hence the prominence of

the sayings of Jesus in the Ibha. *The Revival of the Religious Sciences is seen* as being among the most intuitive accounts of the human heart.[5]

As seen earlier, Ghazali was a Sufi, and he makes clear there are other central figures to take note of, beginning with the greatest example, Muhammad, but also 'Ali and other Sufi saints. However, "Jesus' sayings are dense and rhythmic, constantly reappearing at the high points of Ghazali's moral argument as it ties together a vast array of Hadith."[6]

Various traditions from the time of Muhammad stress a special closeness to Jesus for it is said that no prophet was sent to the interval between them. The Islamic Jesus has been filtered and transmitted in a Muslim environment. Even if we think of this Jesus as an artificial creation, Khalidi writes: ". . . he seems to be an unusual instance of the way in which one religion reaches out to borrow the spiritual heroes of another religion to reinforce its own piety."[7]

Dr. Khalidi's book contains 303 examples of the sayings and stories of Jesus found in Islamic sources. Concerning Jesus, he writes:

> . . . he remains a towering religious figure in his own right – one who easily, almost naturally, rises above two religious environments, the one that nurtured him and the other that adopted him. Amid the current tensions between Christianity and Islam in certain regions of the Middle East and Europe (and, parenthetical, today, in the United States), it is salutary to remind ourselves of an age and a tradition when Christianity and Islam were more open to each other, more aware of and reliant on each other's witness.[8]

Hans Kung agrees with Dr. Khalidi's assessment and feels that the need for dialogue between the world's two largest religions is urgent. He writes:

> Unless the signs of the times are deceiving, despite tremendous political difficulties, the ethnic and religious tensions and violent conflicts, we are at the beginning of new theological conversations which do not deny the well-known differences between the great monotheistic religions but put them in a different light.[9]

In a later chapter, the question of such dialogue will be dealt with more fully. In the next chapter, the history of Christian/Islamic relations will be discussed.

NOTES

1. Tarif Khalidi, *The Muslim Jesus* (Cambridge, Massachusetts: Harvard University Press, 2003).

2. *Ibid.*, 2.
3. *Ibid.*, 29.
4. *Ibid.*, 4.
5. *Ibid.*, 42.
6. *Ibid.*
7. *Ibid.*
8. *Ibid.*, 44.
9. *Ibid.*, 45.

Chapter Eight

Christianity and Islam: Coexistence . . . A Possibility?

Relations between Christianity and Islam have been hostile for fourteen centuries. From the seventh through the fifteenth century, Muslims invaded the Holy Land, Central Europe, Italy, Spain, and North Africa. Christians reacted principally through the Crusades (1095-1291) which resulted in anti-Christian attitudes among Muslims. At the same time, Christian disdain toward Islam intensified.

In the East, the writing of John of Damascus, who died in 750 A.D., is noteworthy. John was a monk in the monastery of St. Sabas in Jerusalem and is regarded as the most important systematic theologian of the Orthodox Church and the last Church Father. In his most important work, *Source of Knowledge*, he presents a negative view of Islam which was widely accepted. Basically, he held that Muhammad was not a genuine prophet and his revelation was a product of his imagination. In effect, Islam was a false religion. The Crusades intensified this negative image.

In the West, for more than four hundred years, Christians had no authentic knowledge of Islam. Paradoxically, the Crusades led to a greater knowledge of the Prophet Muhammad and the teachings of Islam. However, such knowledge was at an academic level. For example, St. Thomas Aquinas in the thirteenth century believed he could defend Christian teachings against Islam at a purely rational level without dealing with the Qur'an or establishing dialogue with Muslim scholars. In 1541, Pope Clement VII had the Arabic text of the Qur'an burnt. At about the same time, Martin Luther called for the translation and publication of the Qur'an, but only so that everyone could see that it was a book filled with lies, fables, and every kind of abomination. Because of the military threat of the Ottoman Turks, Luther referred to the Turkish rulers as servants of the devil, Muhammad as a pseudo-prophet driven by lust, and Islam as a power opposed to Christ. Luther wrote against Islam often. For example: *On War Against the Turks* (1529); *A Campaign Sermon Against the Turks* (1529); *A Book on the Life and Customs of the Turks* (1530); *Appeal to Prayer Against the Turks* (1541); *Brother Richard's Refutation of the Qur'an* (1541).

The nineteenth century and the historical studies of Islam which it produced paved the way for a less polemical assessment of Islam on the part of Christian theology. Nevertheless, colonialism and the military, economic, cultural, and religious expansions of the West during the past two centuries, coupled with the Iraq and Afghanistan wars have led to greater hostility on the part of the Islamic world. The September 11th, 2001, destruction of the World Trade Center and other attacks by al-Qaida (Arabic al-qa'ida = "foundation," "basis") in Europe and elsewhere has engendered great hostility toward Islam in the West. Mutual understanding and dialogue, for the most part, has come to a standstill though efforts are being made to overcome this problem.

Hans Kung, in his book *Islam: Past, Present and Future,* stresses the need for dialogue among the world's great monotheistic religions. As the jacket of this book remarks, no other religion has come under such close scrutiny or been viewed as a source of so much harm to our civilization as Islam. It is routinely portrayed in the media as a promoter of terrorism, supporter of authoritarian governments, oppressor of women, and as enemy of the West. Kung demonstrates that this simplistic perception is far from the reality of Islam. He presents an overview of Islam's 1400-year history and examines its fundamental beliefs and practices, outlines its major schools of thought, and surveys the positions of Islam on the urgent questions of the day. He does so honestly and critically. Above all else, he calls for dialogue and explains the avenues that can be taken in this regard. The goal of such dialogue is more than tolerance, though it is that, but also, and more importantly, mutual respect and ultimately peace among nations.

An excellent book by Dr. Zachary Karabell, *Peace Be With You*, has as its theme the story of Muslim/Christian relations but also includes examples of the manner in which Judaism's coexistence was dealt with by Muslims and Christians.[1]

Dr. Karabell received his undergraduate degree at Columbia University, a master's degree in modern Middle Eastern Studies at Harvard, where he also earned his Ph.D. in 1996. He has taught at Harvard, the University of Massachusetts, and Dartmouth. As a graduate student, he traveled throughout the Middle East. He tells us that when he taught classes on Islam:

I found that my students usually viewed Islam through a dark prism of Muslim hordes threatening to deluge Christendom. The actual stories may have been blurry in their minds, but each time they saw a picture of a mosque or of an imam leading prayer, it struck a deep negative cord: Islam is a religion of violence, and Muslims have clashed with Christians and Jews forever. These beliefs were hardly limited to my students. They are part of our culture.[2]

Dr. Karabell is very clear in showing that Christians, Jews, and Muslims have often lived constructively with one another. While the relationship between Islam and the West can be and often has been fratricidal, it can be and often has been fraternal. Karabell's book is not meant to be a comprehensive history of the past fourteen hundred years. A number of excellent books containing such history have been written. Rather, he concentrates on the periods of concord which are less known to most people. Despite the periods of conflict, which he does not ignore, he describes the less known periods of peace and mutual respect. The lesson for the present and the future is that history shows there is a real possibility of peace and coexistence among Muslims, Christians, and Jews. He realizes that recalling the forgotten history of positive relations between Islam and the West isn't a panacea, but it is a vital ingredient for a more stable, more secure world.

Karabell recounts an interesting period from the Abbasid Empire (750-1258 A.D.) whose capital was in Baghdad. An elite group of Muslims and Christians in the ninth century had serious discussions and relied on reason and philosophy in order to demonstrate the truth of their religions.[3] As Karabell notes: "What also stands out is how much common ground there was, not just between the philosophers, caliphs and theologians, but between Sufis and Christian and Jewish hermit monks."[4] Baghdad had been built on the banks of the Tigris sometime after 760 A.D. by the Abbasid caliph as-Mansur. It became a cosmopolitan city and its openness was marked by the easy toleration of Christians and Jews. Muslim scholars studied the legacy of the Christian states they had conquered as well as classical Greece and the legacy of the Persian shahs. Abbasid caliphs invited Christians, Jews and Zoroastrians to serve the state and many non-Muslims held high administrative posts in the government. However, in the mid-ninth century, this openness to non-Muslims gave way to discrimination as the Abbasid Empire began to fray. The reason for the discriminatory laws against non-Muslims was not animosity toward their religions but as Karabell writes:

> . . . the growing power of Turkish mercenaries, who had become the shock troops for the Abbasids and were becoming a threat to the caliph's authority. The persecution of the People of the Book was only one small element of a major effort to establish a new power base. That effort relied on traditionalists who would not question the caliph and on troops that would serve only him. Marginalizing the People of the Book and suppressing dissent were necessary, albeit cold-blooded tactics.[5]

The switch from tolerance in secure times to intolerance in threatening times occurred time and again in the following centuries. In his introduction, Karabell writes:

Muslim societies had been most tolerant when they have been secure. That is hardly unusual in human affairs, but for most of the past century, few Muslim communities have felt secure. One of the results of September 11 is that Western societies have also become insecure, rationally or not. The result is a rise of intolerance on all sides. Increasingly, more people throughout the world believe that Muslims and Western societies are destined to clash and that they will always clash until one or the other triumphs. That belief is poisonous, and one antidote is the rich historical tradition that says other paths are not only possible but have been taken time and time again.[6]

THE CRUSADES

From its earliest decades, Islam has been locked in a political and religious struggle with Christianity. As we have seen, Muslim armies conquered much of the Mid-East during the seventh century including Persia, Mesopotamia, Syria, Palestine, and Egypt, and in the eighth century parts of India and large parts of Spain and North Africa. By the ninth century, they had captured Sicily and took control of the Mediterranean Sea. Although conversions to Islam were initially slow, by the eleventh century many Christians, living under Muslim rule, had become Muslim. This led to a fear that a similar fate was in store for Europe.

By the beginning of the eleventh century, Christianity's response to Islam took two forms: an attempt to reconquer (the Reconquista) Spain (1000-1492) as well as Italy and Sicily (1061), and the Crusades (1095-1204).

As a prelude to discussing the Crusades, it is important to remember that Jerusalem is a sacred city for all three Abrahamic religions. It was conquered by Arab armies in 638. However, it was and remained a major pilgrimage site for Christians. Christians and their churches were unharmed. Jews, who had been banned from living there by Christians were permitted, under Arab rule, to return and live in the city and to practice their religion. Rather soon after their arrival, Muslims built a shrine, the Dome of the Rock, and the al-Aqsa mosque in the city. From 638 until the First Crusade (1096) the three monotheistic religions lived a relatively peaceful existence in Jerusalem.

Several events which preceded Pope Urban II's call for a crusade are important to recall. In 1009, the Fatimid (Egyptian) caliph, al-Hakim, who was a rather brutal fundamentalist and an erratic ruler, had the Church of the Holy

Sepulchre, built in Jerusalem by Emperor Constantine, torn down. This is one of the events which eventually led to the crusade.

Another important event was the defeat by the Byzantine army in 1071 by a Turkish (Seljuq) army. Fearing that Asia Minor might be overrun, Alexius I, the Byzantine emperor, asked the pope and the Christian kings to aid Constantinople by forming a crusade to liberate Jerusalem and the area surrounding it from Muslim rule.

Jerusalem had been under the rule of one Muslim prince or another since the seventh century, and Christian pilgrims had rarely been denied access to the city. Even the brief onslaught by the rather deranged caliph, al-Hakim, had taken place nearly a century earlier. The motivation for the crusade had less to do with the Muslim control of Jerusalem but rather with the situation in Central and Western Europe.

As many historians have noted, the Crusades proved to be a brilliant solution to the chaos and anarchy of Europe. At the time, the princes of France were engaged in constant battle with one another and the situation in Germany wasn't much better. The church, other than centers like Cluny, functioned at the pleasure of the nobles. In calling for the liberation of Jerusalem, Pope Urban hoped to focus the princes on something other than infighting and thereby increase the prestige and influence of the church. A divided Christendom responded to the Pope's call. Warriors from France, who led the Crusade, and from other parts of Western Europe, united against the "infidel" in a holy war whose goal was to retake the city of Jerusalem. They were called "Franks" not "Crusaders" by the Muslims because most of them were from Frankish lands once ruled by Charlemagne.

The Pope asked the knights to mark themselves as soldiers of Christ by wearing the symbol of the cross, which they willingly did. Pope Urban stated that every believer had a duty to join the Crusade provided they had the means to do so and he said that everyone who answered the call would be rewarded. He is quoted as saying: "All who die by the way, whether by land or by sea, or in battle against the pagans, shall have immediate remission of sin." This I grant through the power of God with which I am invested." Not to partake in this venture, the Pope went on to say, was unacceptable. He wrote:

O what a disgrace if such a despised and base race, which worships demons, should conquer a people that has the faith of omnipotent God and is made glorious with the name of Christ. With what reproaches will the Lord overwhelm us if you do not aid those, who with us, profess the Christian religion! Let those who have been accustomed unjustly to wage private warfare against the faithful now go against the infidels and end with victory which should have been long ago. Let those who have been robbers now become knights. Let those who have been fighting their brothers and sisters now fight in a proper way against the barbarians. Let those who have been serving as mercenaries for small pay now obtain the eternal reward . . . Let those who go not put off the journey, but rent their lands and collect money from their expenses, and as soon as winter is over and spring comes, let them eagerly set out on the way with God as their guide."[7]

The goal of capturing Jerusalem was ironic because as F. E. Peters had observed: "God may have indeed wished it, but there is certainly no evidence that the Christian of Jerusalem did, or that anything extraordinary was occurring to pilgrims there to prompt such a response at that moment in history."[8] Concerning the Crusade, John L. Esposito writes:

In fact, Christian rulers, knights and merchants were driven primarily by political and military ambitions and the promise of economic and commercial (trade and banking) rewards that would accompany the establishment of a Latin kingdom in the Middle East. However, the appeal to religion captured the popular mind and gained its support.[9]

Jerusalem fell to the Crusaders in mid-July, 1099, three long and often bloody years after the Crusade had begun. The Muslim accounts of what occurred describes horrible outrages committed by the Crusaders, and the Christian chroniclers were also shocked at what happened. The city was desecrated and its inhabitants were massacred, and the massacre was not limited to Arab and Turkish Muslims. The Jews of the city and the Eastern Orthodox monks who were protecting the Church of the Holy Sepulchre were also killed. Women and children were killed and many atrocities were reported. Noteworthy is the fact that this was the only crusade which achieved its military aim.

After the "success" of the Crusade, the dome of the Rock was converted into a church and the al-Aqsa mosque became the residence of the Christian king. However, the Latin Kingdom of Jerusalem lasted less than a century. In 1187, Saladin and his army recaptured Jerusalem. Unlike the Crusaders in 1099, the Muslims spared civilians and churches and shrines were left untouched.

The second, third, and fourth major crusades were failures for a variety of reasons. Three other minor crusades were failures as well and were of no historical importance. The fourth major crusade (1202-1204) was initiated by Pope Innocent III. It led to a disastrous conquest and plundering of Eastern Orthodox Constantinople and the establishment of a Latin emperor and of Latin church organization. This crusade sealed the East-West schism which took place in 1054. For fifty years after the sack of Constantinople in 1204, the Latins ruled the imperial city and the Byzantine Emperor was forced into exile. The imperial family returned in the middle of the thirteenth century but when it did so its power had been drastically reduced and its role was more symbolic than real. But Byzantium remained a powerful symbol as the last relic of Rome. On May 29, 1453, Constantinople fell to Sultan Mehmet III and his Ottoman army. The Byzantine capital was renamed Istanbul and became the seat of the Ottoman Empire.

In military terms, the effect of the Crusades was rather negligible. During the twelfth and thirteenth centuries, armies from France, Germany, Italy and England invaded the Near East. Along with the capture of Jerusalem, Crusader states were established, but even at their height they barely contained a narrow stretch that included present day Israel, Lebanon, and small sections of Jordan, Turkey, and Syria. By the beginning of the fourteenth century, the Crusades as a mass movement were over and the Crusaders states were eradicated. Hans Kung remarks concerning the Crusades: "In the glorious history of Islam, the Crusades – however much they remain rooted in Muslim memory as aggression – remain merely episodes which took place on the frontier of the empire and did not shake the power of Islam."[10]

Zachary Karabell is quite right when he observes that "In purely symbolic terms...the Crusades became the perfect metaphor for conflict between Islam and the West. Out of the sorry, often pathetic history of the Crusades, the myth of the endless conflict was forged."[11] The West and Islam have usually described the Crusades in black and white terms, leaving out the many peaceful years of coexistence between Muslims and Christians when actual fighting was not taking place. As Karabell writes:

> In the long years that separated the actual Crusades, Muslims lived uneventfully under Christian rule in the West. While there was far less of the cultural interaction that made Muslim Spain so dynamic, there was also little animosity. Indifference may not be the stuff of legend, but it more accurately describes the decades of live-and-let-live that separated the brief but exciting episodes of armies mustering, sieges laid, and battles fought.[12]

However, as Karabell notes, in regard to the Crusades, we remember the fighting but not the peaceful coexistence. Why? Because describing battles is much more exciting. And though it is true that during the twelfth and thirteenth centuries a year rarely passed without some kind of battle, there were long periods of coexistence.

MUSLIM SPAIN

The clearest example of interreligious tolerance historically speaking was found during the Muslim rule of Spain (al-Andalus) from 756 to approximately 1000. In 711, the Umayyad army crossed into the Iberian (Spanish) peninsula and rapidly conquered most of it. In 750, the Umayyad dynasty was overthrown by the Abbasid dynasty whose capital was Baghdad. In 756, Abd al-Rahman ibn Muawiyah, a Umayyad prince, established himself in Cordoba as ruler of al-Andalus, i.e., those parts of Iberia ruled by Muslims. From 711 until the expulsion of Muslims under King Ferdinand and Queen Isabella in 1492, Cordoba became the locus of the most prolonged encounter between Christianity and Islam.

Some of the finest cultural achievements of Islam occurred in al-Andalus: the great mosque of Cordoba, the Alhambra of Seville, the Cuenca school of ivory carving, the philosophy of Ibn Rushd (Averroes), and the medicine of Ibn Zuhr. The golden age ended in 1016 with the collapse of the Cordoban caliphate.

Other than the extreme north and west, the entire peninsula was ruled from Cordoba. The city was a seat of culture, wealth, commerce, and learning. Muslims were significantly outnumbered by Christians and Spain also had a large Jewish population. Christians and Jews as People of the Book were given the status of dhimmis or persons protected by Muslims. Sabeans, who were monotheists, and at times Zoroastrians and Hindus, were accorded this status. Adult male dhimmis were required to pay a poll tax and at times a tax on their land. In return, they were afforded protective status which included security of life and property, defense against enemies, communal self-government, and freedom of religious practice. Freedom of religion in the modern sense did not exist. There were no equal rights in the modern sense. There were restrictions on the dhimmis such as no Muslims as slaves, no riding on horses, no houses higher than one's Muslim neighbor's houses, no prominent practice of one's own religion, and special clothes had to be worn. People of the Book could not marry Muslims. Jews and Christians could not build synagogues or churches outside of their quarter, but within the quarter they lived in their own world, governed by their own laws and traditions. Even as they adopted Arabic as their primary language, Christians could not avoid the fact that they were second-class citizens in their own country. However, both Christians and Jews occupied prominent positions in society and they benefitted from Cordoba's increasing power and wealth.

Like conquered people throughout history, many Christians of Andalusia were drawn to the power and culture of their conquerors. A good number converted to Islam. There were many great advantages in doing so. As Karabell writes:

> Though a Christian could rise high, there was a limit. A Muslim lord might employ a Christian or a Jew as a minister, and the People of the Book could become

rich and powerful, but they were never allowed to forget that their freedoms were at the mercy of the Muslims who controlled the armies and the treasuries.[13]

Relative to what might have been, nevertheless, Christians enjoyed a rather remarkable freedom. Theological debates and discussions between Muslims, Jews, and Christians were fostered in Spanish Muslim courts. Constructive relations between the three monotheistic religions were promoted in Cordoba. The caliphs of Cordoba, like their brethren in Baghdad, promoted interfaith dialogue. They imitated the prophet Muhammad in this regard, even though the debates were often held in order to prove the other side was wrong. The fact that debate was permitted and even encouraged allowed some degree of open exchange between the faiths and thereby promoted educational and cultural awareness of those involved.

Such interfaith dialogue was not new. Beginning in the time of Muhammad, there are many examples of interfaith dialogue. Muhammad himself dialogued with the Christians of Najran, a city in southern Arabia near the Yemen. In 632, a delegation of sixty Christians came to Medina to make a treaty with the Prophet. This resulted in a mutually agreeable relationship whereby the Najranis were permitted to pray in Muhammad's mosque.

In the next century, Harun al-Rashid (764-809) became the fifth Abbasid Caliph. Baghdad was his capital and the Caliphate reached its apogee during his reign. Open religious debate and discussion was a constant facet of his court. He also fostered learning and promoted poetry. One of the hallmarks of the Abbasid rule was the easy toleration of Christians and Jews. Al-Rahid's son, al-Ma'mum (783-833), succeeded him. He promoted scientific study and the translation of Greek learning into Arabic. He founded a state-funded library in Baghdad called the "House of Wisdom" which was a center for such translation. A medical school was founded during his reign. According to one account, the caliph held a salon every Tuesday afternoon where questions of theology and law were analyzed by Muslims and Christians. Food and drink were served. When the meal ended, discussions began and lasted well into the evening. Al-Ma'mum understood that only in an atmosphere where divergent views were shared could knowledge advance. The historian al-Tabari described an incident when al-Ma'mum hosted a debate between two Muslims. One of the debaters insulted the other. Al-Ma'mum rebuked him, saying: "Hurling insults is unseemly, and unpleasant language is reprehensible. We have allowed theological disputations to take place and have staged the open presentation of religious viewpoints. Now upon whoever speaks the truth, we bestow praise; for whoever does not know the truth, we provide instruction."[14]

THE OTTOMAN EMPIRE

The Ottoman Empire is an outstanding example of the positive treatment of Christians and Jews in a Muslim-controlled context, even though the debates and discussions of earlier times were not as prominent. The empire began in approximately 1300 and continued until its demise in 1923. Its founder was Osman I who headed members of the Ghuzz clan of the Turks. The clan controlled Western Anatolia and in 1357 began a series of conquests which brought Macedonia, Serbia, and Bulgaria under their control. In 1453, under Sultan Mehmet, the city of Constantinople was conquered. The city was besieged for fifty-four days by a Turkish force of 150,000. The defense of the city was in the hands of an army of only 8,000, led by some 400 Venetian mercenaries. The city had been ravaged and depopulated by Latin Crusaders during the Fourth Crusade, who were led by Doge Dandolo of Venice. Obviously, Constantinople was in a weakened condition in 1453. After taking control of the city, Muslim leadership changed its name to Istanbul as was mentioned earlier.

Mehmet, who was faced with an underpopulated capital and insufficient numbers to carry out complicated tasks, ordered thousands of Jews to move to the city. They possessed the skills that the Ottomans needed. Difficult as the relocations were for the Jews, many believe, in hindsight, that living under the Ottomans was a significant improvement over both the Western Christian regions in Europe and the Eastern Christian rulers of Byzantium. By the end of the fifteenth century, the Jews of the city were thriving. After the expulsion on the Jews from Spain in 1492, the Ottomans announced that they would be welcome and receive support, including transportation, if they would move to Istanbul. The Sultan also said he would appreciate it if they would settle in northern Greece, in the city of Thessaloniki, and many did.

The Ottoman Empire reached its height under Sulayman the Magnificent (1520-1566), known as "the lawgiver." He controlled Asia Minor, Syria, Iraq, Egypt, North Africa, the coastal regions of Arabia, Azerbaijan, the Balkans, Hungary, and vassal states in the Volga region and the southern steppes of Russia. Other than his great military successes, his reign saw great achievements in administration, social institutions, architecture, and public works. Istanbul became, once again, one of the great cities of the world.

The religious communities of the Ottoman Empire were organized into millets (from Arabic, millah, "religion" or "religious community"). This policy was established by Mehmet II (1451-81). The Ottomans officially recognized four religious communities as millets: Greek Orthodox, Armenian Gregorian, Muslim, and Jewish. The Christian sects included Maronites in

Lebanon, Copts in Egypt, and Assyrians (also known as Nestorians) in Iraq. Each millet was self-governed and its leader was responsible for assisting the Ottoman state in collecting taxes. Those within a millet were allowed to follow their own civil and religious rules, and were subject to their own religious leaders, who were given official status by the Ottoman administration. In regard to Christian millets, Karabell writes:

> The diverse Christian communities, though rarely satisfied with their status, understood that the autonomy they enjoyed under the Ottoman system was an improvement over what came before. That didn't stop them from competing for influence, and throughout the seventeenth, eighteenth, and nineteenth centuries, Christian millets waged quiet campaigns against one another in provincial courts and in palace chambers in Istanbul. But these internecine conflicts existed under the watchful eye of the Ottoman state, which kept ancient rivalries from spinning out of control and into outright violence. Hatred and resentment festered, but actual frighting was kept to a minimum.

> That fact did not go unnoticed and unappreciated. In the eighteenth century, the Greek patriarch in Jerusalem, who was well acquainted with the struggles between different Christian groups, lauded the Ottomans for all they had done to keep the peace.[15]

The Ottoman Empire crumbled in the late nineteenth and early twentieth centuries for a number of reasons, and the tolerance which had prevailed for so long gave way to Ottoman nationalism and a resultant intolerance. For example, Armenians suffered greatly. The Ottoman Turks were so concerned about Armenian nationalism that they engineered the forced removal of millions of Armenians during World War I, many of whom died or were killed in the process. Christians in the Balkans also underwent brutal attacks at the hands of the Ottomans. But for five centuries, the Ottoman policy had been one of tolerance and coexistence, even though this dissipated at the end of the empire's existence.

In the twentieth century, the Ottoman rule came to an end under the leadership of Mustafa Kemal (1881-1938). He was the first to establish a radical modernized and secularized government in a Muslim nation. He broke all ties with the sultan and the Ottoman regime. In fact, he moved the capital from Istanbul to Ankara as a symbol of this break.

Kemal graduated from the Istanbul military academy and later became a general in the Turkish army. He had a brilliant military career and during World War I he won the admiration of the Turkish people by leading a successful defense of the Dardanelles against the British. In 1920, he convened the Turkish National Assembly in Ankara. Kemal was president and supreme commander. In 1922, a "national assembly" abolished the sultanate. On

April 24, 1923, the Turkish national state was recognized with firmly fixed frontiers. That same year the caliphate, the political and religions institution which had lasted for a millennium, was abolished and in the name of the sovereignty of the people the national assembly proclaimed the Turkish Republic.

Kemal was an atheist. He was uninterested in the Quran and Hadith. He did not seek a reformation of religion but a transformation of society. He wanted a modern secular Turkish society akin to what had occurred in France, which included separation of church and state. Hans Kung describes the constitution passed on April 24, 1924, which contains six principles sponsored by Kemal, which made Turkey a thoroughly modern state in the following way:

> The principles of action were nationalism (the nation state), secularism (laicism), and modernism (the emancipation of women and the abolishment of the prohibition of alcohol), and the principles of organization were republicanism (the form of government), populism (the sovereignty of the people), and statism (a controlling role of the state in the economy, state capitalism, and modern legislation on work and social welfare).[16]

Kemal dictatorially introduced a new legal system which became the foundation of the revolutionary change in Turkey. He introduced the Swiss civil law book which was translated into Turkish and passed by the parliament with few changes. The changes which followed impacted all of Turkey, the urban middle class as well as rural villagers. Among these changes, Swiss family and divorce laws were extended to women as well as granting women the right to vote and to work in the professional world. Wearing the veil was no longer required. The Westernization and secularization process also included the international reckoning of time (the Gregorian calendar) together with new weights and measures. New music and architecture were promoted, new universities and schools were founded, and theatres and concert halls were built. Among the reforms, Islamic forms of dress were abolished, and in 1928, Arabic script was replaced with Latin script. Kemal believed that eighty percent of Turks were illiterate because they could not understand Arabic characters. Arabic and Persian were removed from school curricula. All newspapers and books were commanded to use Latin script. At the same time, Kemal promoted Turkish identity. They were, after all, Turks, not Arabs. Because of this, in 1934, the National Assembly gave him the title "Attaturk," "Father of the Turks." To the present day, portraits and memorials of Kemal are displayed in school rooms, restaurants, public institutions, and squares, in private homes, and elsewhere. He is honored today as in 1934 as the "Father of the Turks."

The entire Arab world, both conservatives and liberals, is following developments in Turkey closely. The example of Turkey is very important. The fact that Turkey has become a democratic system, as well as modern and secular, and yet Islam continues to predominate is, to say the least, noteworthy.

NOTES

1. Zachary Karabell, *Peace Be Upon You* (New York: Alfred A. Knopf, 2007).

2. *Ibid.*, 2.

3. See Sidney Griffith, *The Beginning of Christian Theology in Arabic: Muslim-Christian Encounters in the Early Islamic Period* (Burlington, Vermont: Ashgate, 2002), 15ff.

4. Karabell, *op. cit.*, 6.

5. *Ibid.*, 56.

6. *Ibid.*, 9.

7. From the account written by Robert the Monk which can be found on the Internet Medieval Source-Book at www.Fordham.edu/halsall/shook1k.html.

8. F. E. Peters, *Allah's Commonwealth: A History of the Near East* (New York: Simon and Schuster, 1973), 85).

9. Esposito, *Islam: The Straight Path, op. cit.*, 64.

10. Kung, *op. cit.*, 310.

11. Karabell, *op. cit.*, 87.

12. *Ibid.*, 88.

13. *Ibid.*, 67.

14. See Marshall C. S. Hodgson, *The Venture of Islam,* Vol. 1 (Chicago: University of Chicago Press, 1974), 462-463.

15. Karabell, *op. cit.*, 183.

16. Kung, *op. cit.*, 435.

Chapter Nine

Muslims in North America

Substantial numbers of Muslims arrived in what is now the United States as slaves in the early 1600s, and this status continued until the abolition of slavery in 1863. Scholars estimate that somewhere between fourteen and twenty percent of African slaves were Muslim. In the twentieth century and continuing to the present, African Americans have studied their cultural and spiritual heritage. This, and other factors, has led a number of African Americans to embrace Islam. It is estimated that as many as a third of the Muslim population in the United States today is African American.

Muslims from the Middle East began arriving in America in the late nineteenth century. This first "wave" were from the Syrian regions of the Arab world and for the most part were unskilled and uneducated laborers, as were many other immigrants from European countries. Following World War I, many more Arab immigrants arrived, representing a second "wave" who were also, for the most part, unskilled laborers. The third "wave" of immigrants, mostly from the Arab countries but also from Eastern Europe and the Soviet regions, were generally better educated and more skilled than the earlier waves.[1] Economic factors have always been central in the lives of those who have immigrated to America, but in regard to the third wave, the desire to escape political oppression and persecution was critical. That this group of Muslims is well educated is not surprising since immigrants from many countries, representing many religious traditions, and often well educated, have been immigrating to the United States since 1967 when new U.S. immigration laws took effect. Approximately one million immigrants are welcomed legally every year.

Immigrant Muslims outnumber all other Muslims, followed by African American Muslims, and then by indigenous others, mostly white, middle-class people. What is most interesting is the fact that there is a bewildering diversity of Muslims from around the world now living in the United States. As Frederich Mattewson Denny observes:

> The majority of immigrant Muslims have come from the Arab world, South Asia (Afghanistan, Bangladesh, India, and Pakistan), Iran and Turkey. But some Islamic Centers, such as the Islamic Center of Greater Toledo, in Ohio, and the Islamic Center of Southern California, in Los Angeles, have more than thirty different nationalities and ethnicities represented in their membership.[2]

Denny observes that "It is ironic that a microcosm of the global umma should find its first realization in an environment that is non-Islamic, pluralistic, free, and highly secularized.

Presently it is unclear as to the number of Muslims in the United States. In 2001, the Council on American-Islamic Relations (CAIR), a Muslim advocacy group, used a common assumption that only one in three Muslims are associated with a mosque. To CAIR, this suggests that there are at least six million Muslims in the country. Surveys conducted by non-Muslims estimate only three million. As a result, estimates vary greatly between three to six million, though six million seems to be more accurate, especially if the estimates are based solely on Mosque attendance. It is safe to say that the Muslim population will continue to grow due to immigration and higher birthrates and to a lesser extent due to conversions, especially among African Americans.

Like other Americans, Muslims generally live in cities and suburbs with large numbers in New York, Chicago, Detroit, and Los Angeles. Overall they are quite successful. As Paul M. Barrett writes:

> Surveys show that the majority of Muslims are employed in technical, white-collar, and professional fields. These include information technology, corporate management, medicine, and education. An astounding 59 percent of Muslim adults in the United States have college degrees. That compares with only 27 percent of all American adults. Four out of five Muslims earn at least twenty-five thousand dollars a year; more than half earn fifty thousand dollars or more. A 2004 survey by a University of Kentucky researcher found that median family income among Muslims is sixty thousand dollars a year; the national median is fifty thousand. Most Muslims own stock or mutual funds, either directly or through retirement plans. Four out of five are registered to vote.[3]

There are an estimated 1,300 mosques in the United States and several hundred religious schools. In the past, imams and other religious teachers were brought in from foreign countries but they were not always sensitive to the problems of daily life that their congregations encountered. As a result, beginning in the 1980s, the training of imams has been seriously undertaken in the United States. Also, legal councils which specifically address life in

America have been founded in order to respond to questions raised by local communities. Again, beginning in the 1980s, Muslims have made a concerted effort to participate in interfaith activities with Jews and Christians.

An interesting article appeared in *USA Today* on September 25, 2007 (pp. 1a and 1b) concerning the growing diversity of the Muslim community in the United States which, in fact, due to certain tensions between some Shi'ites and Sunnis, is challenging the tradition of assimilation which has taken place for many within the two groups. Cathy Lynn Grossman, the author of the article, notes that for years many Sunnis and Shi'ites have worked together to build mosques, support charities, register voters, and hold well attended celebrations for Eid al Fitr, the feast at the end of the holy month of Ramadan. Now, however, there are small signs of tension emerging in the American Muslim community that are raising concerns among many of its leaders. They worry that the bitter divisions that have caused so much trouble abroad, for example between Shi'ites and Sunnis in Iraq, are beginning to have an impact here, at least among some Muslims.

Doctor Ingrid Mattson is a professor of Islamic Studies at Hartford Seminary in Hartford, Connecticut, and the president of the largest Muslim civic and social group in the United States, the Islamic Society of North America. At the society's annual Labor Day weekend gathering at Rosemont, a Chicago suburb, which was part academic seminar, part community rally, and part reunion for more than 30,000 families, Mattson's keynote speech urged Muslims "to look beyond the seventh century tribal society into which Islam was revealed." Her intent was for all Muslims to find common ground, which is ample, and to love and respect one another. Dialogue is paramount for this to happen.

Grossman points out that for all the conflict abroad among Muslims, those in America have not only gotten along, but many have assimilated. She observes that in a 2006 survey of 1,000 registered voters, about 12 percent identified themselves as Shi'ites, 36 percent said they were Sunni, and 40 percent called themselves "just a Muslim," according to the Council of American-Islamic Relations (CAIR). Ibrahim Hooper, a CAIR spokesman, stated "America gives people the unique opportunity to leave cultural, historical baggage behind. We can serve as a model to the world of Islam that is clear, calm, articulate, forthright, and civil."

Besides the efforts to encourage dialogue, there is another phenomenon that could overcome sectarian friction here – the inexorable force of assimilation. Just as a rising number of American Protestants are attending non-denominational community churches and referring to themselves simply as Christians rather than Baptists, Methodists, or Lutheran, for example, a similar occurrence is taking place among many Muslims in the United States.

Eboo Patel, author of *Acts of Faith: The Story of an American Muslim*, a Shi'ite who is married to a Sunni, says they want their child to grow up "fluent in all the multiple rituals and practices of Islam." Grossman quotes him as saying, "The bulk of the American Muslim community is overwhelmingly young, under the age of 40. And they are, according to Patel, experiencing a huge momentum toward "big-tent Islam."[4]

Salim Al-Maragati, executive director of the Muslim Public Affairs Council, states, as quoted by Grossman: "We don't want to be defined by the classifications of history and the Middle East. The Quran is our authority." He calls himself a "Sushi," the popular term for a combination of Sunni and Shi'ite. Once the glib nickname for the children of intermarried couples, it has become the shorthand for Muslims who blur sectarian lines.

At the Labor Day gathering in question there were Sunni and Shi'ite book stands, and booths for major Muslim political and social groups. Imam Muhammad Magid of the All Dulles Area Muslim Society (ADAMS), which has seven mosques in the Washington, D.C. area, says he was heartened when 10,000 people at the Labor Day gathering cheered for a new Code of Honor, pledging Sunni and Shi'ite respect and cooperation. Much is happening to bring this about.

THE NATION OF ISLAM

In 1930, a peddler, whether from Iran, Turkey, or Saudi Arabia is not certain, began preaching in Detroit. His name was Wallace D. Fard. His audience was African American. He preached a message of black liberation. His sources were the Quran and the Bible. He was called the Great Mahdi, or messiah. He taught that blacks were not American and owed no loyalty to the government. Prominent in his teachings were the rejection of Christianity and the domination of blacks by white "blue-eyed devils." He stressed the "religion of the Black Man" and the "Nation of Islam."

After Fard mysteriously disappeared in 1934, Elijah Poole (1897-1975) took over under the name Elijah Muhammad. He built the Nation of Islam into a national movement which he governed in an absolute manner until his death. He emphasized a self-sufficient mentality and a program for self-improvement and empowerment. He focused on Black pride, strong family values, hard work, discipline, thrift, and abstention from gambling, alcohol, drugs, and pork. By the 1970s, the Nation of Islam had more than one hundred thousand members. The "Black Muslims," as they came to be called, promised the fall of the white racist American society and the restoration of the righteous black community. The Nation of Islam assumed the supremacy of blacks. Whites were regarded as devils. As Frederich Mattewson Denny observes, "Although mostly poor people joined and found new lives of dedication and accomplishment, upper-class blacks also joined and provided the movement with a modicum of respectability among the African American community."

The Nation of Islam differed in many respects from traditional Islam. Elijah Muhammad taught that Wallace D. Fard was Allah and thus God was a black man. He also taught that he, Elijah Muhammad, not the prophet Muhammad, was the last messenger of God. He taught that a black separatism rather than Islam's teaching on the brotherhood of all believers, transcending social, tribal, and ethnic differences. Nor did the Nation of Islam observe the Five Pillars of Islam or important Muslim rituals. In addition, mosques were called temples and leaders were called ministers rather than imams.

One of Elijah Muhammad's most important ministers was Malcolm Little (1925-1965), a former convict. He learned about the Nation of Islam in prison, converted, and turned his life around. He became known as Malcolm X, thus ridding himself of his white "slave" name. The "X" refers to the fact that he was an ex-drinker, ex-smoker, ex-thief, ex-slave, ex-Christian. Malcolm was a charismatic speaker and became the most prominent spokesman of the movement and drew many to join the Nation. He came to represent the radical black power movement in the United States by the early 1960s. He militantly challenged the white establishment and was a stark contrast to Reverend Martin Luther King, Jr., who preached nonviolence in the struggle for racial justice. Malcolm preached nationally and internationally. He became friends with a number of Sunni Muslims which led to a gradual change in his thinking, away from that of Elijah Muhammad and toward mainstream Islam.

In 1964, Malcolm X resigned from the Nation of Islam. That same year he went on pilgrimage (hajj) to Mecca. He describes this experience in his autobiography. He was deeply affected by what he witnessed, the equality of all believers regardless of color or nationality. He also became aware that he did not know how to observe the five times of daily prayer and that he had not been taught other prescribed practices found in the Five Pillars of Islam. This awareness led him to accept authentic Islam and he became a Sunni Muslim. When he returned to New York, he took the name El Hajj Malik El-Shabazz. He founded the Muslim Mosque, Inc. in New York City and changed his thinking on black nationalism, which he now rejected. He now taught pan-Africanism, which aligns African Americans with their cultural and religious ties in Africa. Unfortunately, on February 21, 1965, he was assassinated as he spoke to an audience in New York City by two members of the Nation of Islam who were convicted of the murder. Nevertheless, Malcolm X's reputation as a courageous proponent of radical justice and civil rights has grown steadily, and he is now regarded as one of the twentieth century's most significant Muslim reformers. His example has led many African Americans to accept Islam.

In 1975, Elijah Muhammad died and was succeeded by his son Wallace (Warith) Deen Muhammad, as had been designated by his father. Wallace Muhammad quickly and decisively made major teaching reforms in doctrines and organizational structure, which conformed to the teachings of orthodox Sunni Islam. For example, temples were renamed mosques, their leaders were now called imams rather than ministers, the community now learned and observed the Five Pillars of Islam, and the equality of male and female members were taught. In 2003, Wallace Muhammad resigned as leader of the approximately 1.5 million member organization, currently known as the American Society of Muslims. The community continues to flourish. Wallace Muhammad died in 2008.

The Nation of Islam continues to exist under the leadership of Louis Farrakan. He and a minority of the Nation's membership opposed the reforms ushered in by Wallace D. Muhammad. Farrakan, who is a charismatic speaker, bitterly rejected the changes. He believes that he and his followers have remained faithful to the original teachings of Elijah Muhammad, which includes black nationalist and separatist doctrines. Farrakan's militant and anti-Semitic statements have been widely criticized. On the other hand, he has been praised for fighting crime and the use of drugs, as well as for his efforts to rehabilitate prisoners. He has also been lauded for his leadership of the Million Man March in Washington, D.C. in 1995. In recent years, Farrakan has moved the Nation closer to more Orthodox Islamic practices and has maintained a closer identity with mainstream Islam.

NOTES

1. See Yvonne Yazbeck Haddad, *A Century of Islam in America*, "The Muslim World Today," Occasional Paper No. 4 (Washington, D.C.: The Middle East Institute, 1986).

2. Frederich Mattewson Denny, *op. cit.*, 353.

3. Eboo Patel, *Acts of Faith: The Story of an American Muslim* (Boston: Beacon Press, 2007).

4. Denny, *op. cit.*, 354.

Chapter Ten

Radical Islam

Since 9/11, the Wahhabi movement has been accused by governments and the media, among others, as the major Islamic threat facing the United States and Western civilization in general. It is also seen as the inspiration for Osama bin Laden and his al-Qaida network.

Natana J. De Long-Bas, who is a senior research assistant at the Center for Muslim-Christian understanding at Georgetown University, challenged these assumptions in her excellent book, *Wahhabi Islam*, which was published by Oxford University Press in 2004. Among the many negative portrayals, Wahhabism has become infamous for what is perceived as its negative influence on Islam. De Long-Bas points out that Wahhabism has been described as "extremist, radical, puritanical, contemptuous of modernity, misogynist, and militant in nature."[1]

Wahhabism is the creed of the ruling family of Saudi Arabia and has been defended by noted twentieth century reformers such as Muhammad Rashid Rida of Egypt and the Palestinian American scholar Ismail Raji al-Faruqi as a model for reforming Islam in the modern era. DeLong-Bas writes:

> Also at odds with such negative stereotypes are the more positive images of Wahhabis distributing copies of the Quran and hadith (accounts of the sayings and deeds of the prophet), funding hospitals, orphanages, and other charitable institutions; and constructing mosques worldwide.[2]

She goes on to point out how little attention is given to the written works of Wahhabism's founder and ideologue, Muhammad Ibn Abd al-Wahhab (1703-1792). Her book is an attempt to correct this situation. DeLong-Bas's research into the writings of Ibn Abd al-Wahhab was supported by a number of people and she expresses her thanks especially to Dr. Fahd al-Semmari,

Director of the King Abd all-Aziz Foundation for Research and Archives in Riyadh, Saudi Arabia, for making Muhammad Ibn Abd al-Wahhab's writings available to her. Hers is the first study ever undertaken of the writings of the founder: a biography of the Prophet Muhammad; a collection of juridical opinions; a series of exegetical commentaries; and a variety of other works.

DeLong-Bas presents the most comprehensive study of Ibn Abd al-Wahhab's interpretation of jihad ever written. He believed that jihad is strictly limited to the self-defense of the Muslim community against military aggression. She argues that contemporary extremists such as Osama bin Laden do not have their basis on his writings. The cult of martyrdom, the strict division of the world into two necessarily opposing spheres (Muslim and non-believers), the wholesale destruction of civilian life and property, and the call for global jihad are entirely absent in Ibn Abd al-Wahhab's writings. Rather, the militant stance of contemporary jihadism is found in adherence to the writings of the medieval scholar, Ibn Taymiyyah (1263-1328), and the twentieth century Egyptian radical, Sayyid Qutb (1906-1966).

Nevertheless, it is clear that Ibn Abd al-Wahhab preached a stark and puritanical form of Islam which characterized many elements deriving from Sufism and Shi-ism as apostasy. The primary objectives of his wrath were the veneration of Sufi men and women, the idea of saints, visible adornments upon mosques and sacred structures, funeral markers, and ritual practices that detracted from a complete focus on God alone. The Wahhabis believe that all Muslims who did not agree with them were unbelievers and should be subdued (if necessary, killed) in the name of Islam. Central to their theology was the doctrine of God's unity (tawhid), an absolute monotheism. As the Prophet Muhammad destroyed the variety of pre-Islamic gods which surround the Ka'ba in 630 and restored it to the worship of one true God, Allah, the Wahhabis destroyed the sacred tombs of Muhammad and his Companions in Mecca and Medina as well as the pilgrimage site at Karbala in modern Iraq which contained the tomb of Hussein (the son of Ali and Fatima and the grandson of the Prophet Muhammad,) who was killed there in 680. The destruction of the site contributed to the historic antipathy between the Wahhabis of Saudi Arabia and Shi'ite Islam in both Saudi Arabia and Iran.

Islam is the state religion in Saudi Arabia and the Qur'an is interpreted according to the teachings of Wahhabi theology. In 1744, Muhammad ibn Saud founded the first Saudi dynasty in Arabia. He fashioned a politico-religious treaty at that time with Muhammad Ibn Abd al-Wahhab to establish the country on strict Islamic practices with an emphasis on strict monotheism. The alliance of Ibn Abd al-Wahhab as religious head and Muhammad Ibn Saud as political and military head was sealed by the marriage of Ibn Abd al-Wahhab to the daughter of Muhammad ibn Saud. In 1813, Muhammad Ali of Egypt defeated the Saudis in battle and took over the country, but the Saudi movement continued. The Saudis eventually regained control and made Riyadh its new capital. The Saudis were driven out of Riyadh in 1891 by the Rashid of Ha'il clan, fellow Muslims who did not support the Wahhabi cause. In 1901, Abd al-Aziz Al Saud dramatically recaptured Riyadh with a handful of companions in a daring raid, and since then the Saudi dynasty has grown with great success.

DeLong-Bas, in discussing Wahhabism in relation to Osama bin Laden and other modern radicals, makes a number of important points of comparison. She notes that Ibn Abd al-Wahhab placed great importance on education so that Muslims could intelligently engage others in debate about their beliefs in the hope of converting them. She writes: "That he chose to do so by educational means—dialogue, discussion, and debate—rather than the more militant methods, such as conversions of the sword, is particularly noteworthy in the light of standard stereotypes of Wahhabis as militant, violent, and destructive."[3] Ibn Abd al-Wahhab's vision of the world "was not one in which Muslims could only coexist peacefully with other Muslims but rather one in which Muslims were expected to coexist and even cooperate peacefully with others, even though their religious beliefs and practices might differ."[4] On the other hand, bin Laden and other contemporary extremists preach a global jihad of cosmic proportions and the killing of all infidels together with the destruction of their money and property. And bin Laden requires no justification for jihad other than the declaration that the other is an infidel. Ibn Abd al Wahhab's notion of jihad was limited geographically and of localized importance. Jihad had to be defensive (with some exceptions) and its goal was to establish a treaty which would allow peaceful coexistence. Nor did he glorify martyrdom as do radicals today. He believed that the only reason one should participate in jihad was defense of the Muslim community and not the desire for personal reward, whether in this life or in the hereafter.

DeLong-Bas offers other points of serious difference between the teaching of Ibn Abd al-Wahhab and Osama bin Laden and other extremists. She writes: "Although it is often posited that bin Laden's ideology of global jihad has its origins in Ibn Abd al-Wahhab's writings because both are Wahhabis, the reality is that bin Laden's ideology owes far more to the writings of the medieval scholar Ibn Taymiyya and his contemporary interpreter, Sayyid Qutb, than it does to the writings of Ibn Abd al-Wahhab."[5]

Ahmad ibn Taymiyyah was born in Syria in 1263. The area had already succumbed to the Mongol invasion. He came of age at a time when the Mongols, rather than moving on to other conquests, had begun to settle in Muslim lands and to adopt Islam as their religion. They absorbed Islamic beliefs and practices into their own shamanistic spiritual system, creating a kind of hybrid of Sunni Islam and Eastern paganism. The question for Muslims was this: should the people who had killed millions of Muslims and had plundered their land, and who now ruled as Muslims be obeyed? Ibn Taymiyyah's answer was given in the form of a fatwa (an official religious ruling). Concerning the Mongols, he said they were unbelievers and hypocrites who did not really believe in Islam and that every type of hypocrisy, unbelief, and outright rejections of the faith was to be found among them. He added that they were among the most ignorant of all people, who knew little of the Islamic teachings and were far from observing the tenets of Islam. In short, they were apostates and need not be obeyed. His fatwa labeled them as unbelievers (kafirs) who were thus excommunicated (takfir).

What made the fatwa extraordinary was that it violated the most basic tenet of Hanbali doctrine, established by the founder of the Hanbali school of law, Ahmad ibn Hanbali (780-855), which stated that the leader of the Islamic state, whether a caliph, a sultan, or an imam, had been placed in his exalted position by God and thus had to be obeyed regardless of his action or his piety. For ibn Hanbal, social order had to be maintained at all costs. No matter how "unislamic" the actions of a Muslim leader might appear, his rule must be obeyed.

Ibn Taymiyyah disagreed. He felt that to live freely and justly as Muslims required a leader committed to the teachings of Islam. If that leader failed to uphold Muslim principles and did not abide by Islamic law, then he was not really a Muslim but an infidel and his rule was invalid. Ibn Taymiyyah declared that it was incumbent upon all Muslims who were ruled by an impious leader to rebel. Using the practice of takfir, he also taught that any Muslim who was willing to accept the rule of a kafir (unbeliever) leader was himself an unbeliever.

There was precedent for such an extremist view. Six hundred years earlier, a sect called the Kharijites expressed a similar viewpoint when they rebelled against the leadership of the third caliph, Uthman ibn Affan. They did so because they believed that the leader of the Muslim community must be blameless and without sin and must exceed all other Muslims in his piety and learning. If not, he had no right to lead the community and must be removed from power by any means necessary. Ibn Taymiyyah was not a Kharijite but he stressed the obligation of every Muslim to ensure the purity of the community by purging it of all innovation and heresy. He also copied the Kharijite geographical division of the world into realms of belief (dar al-Islam) and unbelief (dar al-kufr). He focused his attention strictly on the enemy living inside dar al-Islam (the land of Islam), that is, on those Muslims who did not adequately follow Islamic law. He considered such individuals heretics. This was especially true of the Shi'ah whom ibn Taymiyyah despised and of the

Mongols who, in his view, were apostates against whom it was incumbent upon all Muslims to declare jihad.

Ibn Taymiyyah contradicted centuries of consensus among his earlier legal scholars by urging that jihad was an individual rather than a collective obligation. Traditionally, jihad had been seen (and still is) as a defensive struggle against oppression and injustice that could be authorized only by a qualified imam or head of state, but for ibn Taymiyyah jihad was an offensive weapon that could be used on one's own and without guidance in order to purify Islam and make it prevail globally. He saw jihad as the highest form of devotion. In his book, *The Religious and Moral Doctrine of Jihad*, he wrote: "It is the best voluntary act that man can perform...it is better than the hajj (the greater pilgrimage) and the 'umrah (lesser pilgrimage), better than voluntary salat (prayer) and voluntary fasting."

Ibn Taymiyyah spent many years in prison for his writings and died there in 1328. For most scholars, his opinions regarding what he called "apostate rulers," together with some of his other ideas, were seen as dangerous and far too radical. His ideas were more or less forgotten for six hundred years but were resurrected in the tumultuous period of post-colonial Egypt and were revived once more by a group of radical Islamists, and most notably by Sayyid Qutb. Through the writings of Qutb, the opinions of ibn Taymiyyah remain relevant today and have inspired the military and religious world view of organizations such as Osama bin Laden's al-Quaeda network.

The question, then, is who is Sayyid Qutb (1906-1966) and what is the relationship of bin Laden's thought to his writing? Qutb was raised in the Egyptian village of Mushya and was educated in the Quran as a youngster. He had memorized the Quran by the time he was ten years old. In 1929, he moved to Cairo to study and in the 1930s and 1940s he was a literary critic and author as well as a teacher in the Ministry of Public Education. From 1948 to 1950, he lived in the United States in order to study the American educational system. In 1949, he studied at Colorado State Teachers College, now the University of Northern Colorado in Greeley, Colorado, which is about 100 miles north of Denver. In the middle of the 20th century, Greeley was a very conservative town, where alcohol was illegal. The founding fathers of Greeley were by all reports temperate, religious and peaceful people. But by the time Qutb returned to Egypt, he was disillusioned by what he perceived as the vices of American society. He felt that the secularism and materialism of American society had resulted in moral laxity and racism, among other vices. He said these vices were due to the lack of religion as a guiding force in American public life. He condemned America as a soulless, materialistic country that no Muslim should live in. It seems that Qutb used this critique to warn Egyptians about the dangers of Western values and of modernity which were attractive to many of his fellow citizens.

When he returned to Egypt he joined the Muslim Brotherhood, which had been founded in Egypt in 1928 by Hasan al-Banna. This was an organization promoting the Islamization of Egyptian society at every level. The Brotherhood joined a group known as the Free Officers, led by Gamal al-Nasser, with the goal of achieving full independence from Britain. In 1952, they overthrew the pro-British monarch. However, whereas the Brotherhood was Islamist in its ideology, Nasser and the Free Officers were staunchly secular and their ideology was that of Arab nationalism. They blamed religion for the lack of progress of contemporary Egyptian society and attempted to remove it from any influence on public life. In 1954, a failed assassination attempt on Nasser was blamed on the Brotherhood, though this was never proven. Nasser used this accusation to obliterate the Brotherhood. Qutb by then was one of its leaders and its dominant intellectual figure. Most of the Brotherhood's leaders, including Qutb, were arrested by Nasser's regime and sentenced to long prison terms, accompanied by torture and degradation. These experiences led to Qutb's radicalization. While in prison he wrote prolifically. In 1965, he was released from prison but was rearrested after the publication of his most famous work, *Milestones.*[6] He was falsely charged with attempting to assassinate Nasser and was convicted and executed the following year.

MILESTONES: SAYYID QUTB

Qutb's formative experiences in developing his teachings of radical Islam resulted from his persecution by the Egyptian government. He knew that many fellow Muslims had also been imprisoned, tortured, and at times put to death by the government. He firmly believed that these and similar actions in other countries resulted from the fact that Muslim nations were no longer governed by Muslim laws (Shariah) and therefore were apostate. True Muslims were in the minority and had an obligation to work for an authentic Muslim society.

In *Milestones*, the book that has greatly impacted radical Islamic thought, his fundamental point is that all ideologies other than Islam, be it Arab nationalism, socialism, democracy, or communism, have demonstrated their bankruptcy. He states that Islam is not manifest in present day society other than in the hearts of true believers. He writes that the present situation is similar to the pre-Islamic period of jahiliyya (ignorance or barbarism). Therefore, Muslims must revive Islam and fight present day jahiliyya.

Milestones describes the cosmic battle between good and evil and presents an outline of a global order and how this can be achieved. He supports his ideology with verses from the Quran and hadith. Given his focus, it is not surprising that a substantial part of his teaching deals with jihad. For Qutb, jihad as holy war was the tool of "Quranic Revolution."[7] It was intended to be a global effort, applicable to all. Its purpose was to create "an organized and embattling army which had to fight the jahilyah."[8] Qutb believed the world is divided into two distinct branches: Dar al-Islam (the territory of Islam), where Islam and shariah were supreme; and Dar al-Jahilizzah (territory of ignorance), where ignorance reigned.

Whereas Ibn Abd al-Wahhab preserved Muhammad's example of engaging in commerce with Jews and Christians, this is certainly not the case with Qutb. As DeLong-Bas writes:

> Qutb rejected outright any kind of relationship with Jews and Christians other than that of jihad. He held "Zionist Jews" and "Christian Crusaders" responsible for the ills of contemporary society and he saw them because of their purported long historical conspiracy to annihilate Islam—a vision consistent with his belief in the ongoing cosmic battle between good and evil.[9]

Qutb accused the "poisonous" Jews of being overly focused on ritual to the exclusion of spirituality, eternally ungrateful to God, and vicious and arrogant when in power, as evidenced by their perfidy, greed, and never-ending conspiracies and plots against Muhammad and the early Muslim community. For Qutb, Zionism was merely the logical conclusion of Jewish history and the centuries-old campaign by the Jews to destroy Islam.

Christians, on the other hand, were blamed for the separation of existence into two mutually exclusive spheres—the sacred and the secular—and the removal of divine law from religion.

In regard to the defensive nature of jihad, Qutb expanded the nature of defense from that of self-protection against military aggression to "defense of man against all the factors and motives which demolish the freedom of man or serve as impediments in the way of his real freedom, particularly when that factor is a political system."[10] When Qutb speaks of freedom, he is not referring to making a personal choice that would reject Islam. In fact, he assumed that jihad would create an atmosphere where people would choose Islam. He believed that "freedom" would offer a person two choices—conversion or submission to Islam. If a person chooses to resist these choices, they are therefore resisting Islam and subject to conversion by the sword or the death penalty.

DeLong-Bas notes that Qutb's vision of global jihad developed during Nasser's secular rule of Egypt and his government's persecution of the

Muslim Brotherhood. As a result, his ideas have inspired radical jihad organizations who see themselves in similar battles with their governments. She writes:

> Qutb's absolute vision of right and wrong and what is to be done about it provides a prescription for active resolution of the problems facing the contemporary Muslim world—a return to religion in which the sovereignty of God alone is recognized and all-out, permanent warfare is waged against any and all who fail to recognize that sovereignty.[11]

OSAMA BIN LADEN

Sayyid Qutb's writings had a great impact on Osama bin Laden, the founder of Al –Quaeda (the "base" or "foundation" of jihad). Bin Laden fought against the Soviets in Afghanistan in the 1980s. His experience during the Afghan jihad had a profound effect on him and led him to adopt the policy of global jihad. He and his followers felt their victory over the Soviets was a sign of the righteousness of their cause. Sayyid Qutb's writings provided the theoretical justification for the path he had taken.

Sayyid Qutb's brother Muhammad is a very important figure in the scenario. He moved to Saudi Arabia following his release from prison in Egypt and became a professor of Islamic Studies. He also edited, published, and promoted his brother's writings. One of Muhammad Qutb's students and an ardent follower of Sayyid's writings was Ayman Zawahiri who became a member of the Egyptian Islamic jihad as well as the mentor of Osama bin Laden and a leading member of al-Quaeda. Bin Laden himself regularly attended weekly public lectures by Muhammad Qutb at King Abdulaziz University and read Sayyid Qutb's writings. The latter's influence on bin Laden is clear in that he rejects all secular ideologies and maintains that secular principles should never predominate over the teachings of Islam. Bin Laden also believes that there is ongoing cosmic conflict between good and evil, between true Muslims and infidels, which requires an unconditional jihad, one which is permanent, in which every true believer has an obligation to participate.

Bin Laden returned to Saudi Arabia after the Afghan War but was not given a hero's welcome. In 1990, when Saddam Hussein invaded Kuwait, he proposed to the Saudi government that he would gather his mujahidin ("freedom fighters") to protect Saudi Arabia. The Saudi Arabian government did not take his proposal seriously and instead invited the United States to do so. This angered bin Laden and turned him against the Saudi royal family. He was exiled by the Saudis in 1992 and took refuge in Sudan. This interlude ended in 1996 when he was exiled from Sudan. He then returned to Afghanistan and, having settled there, he called for jihad against the United States. Originally his call was to remove American troops from Saudi Arabia but later he expanded to include all Americans, wherever they lived. This is not what Ibn Abd al-Wahhab called for in dealing with non-Muslims. He called for dialogue and never spoke of global jihad.

Osama bin Laden's three major problems with the United States are America's military presence in Saudi Arabia, its destructive role in Iraq and Afghanistan and its support of Israel.

To carry out his agenda, bin Laden stresses the idea of martyrdom. Martyrdom operations, in fact, are a rather recent phenomenon in Islam. In Sunni Islam, suicidal attacks are rare prior to the early 1990s. Suicide is strictly forbidden in Islam. For example, Surah 4:29 reads: "...nor kill (or destroy) yourself: for verily Allah has been to you most merciful."

Contemporary radical authorities define martyrdom in the following manner:

> Martyrdom or self-sacrifice operations are those performed by one or more people, against enemies far outstripping them in numbers and equipment, with prior knowledge that the operations will almost inevitably lead to death.[12]

David Cook, in *Understanding Jihad*, writes that radical Muslims find it very important to distinguish the issue of martyrdom from any hint of its similarity to suicide. He quotes from "The Islamic Ruling on the Permissibility of Martyrdom Operations," authored by a "Council of Scholars from the Arabian Peninsula." They write:

> The name "suicide operations" used by some is inaccurate, and in fact this name was chosen by the Jews to discourage people from such endeavors. How great is the difference between one who commits suicide—because of his unhappiness, lack of patience, and weakness, or absence of imam (faith)—and the self-sacrificer who embarks on the operation out of strength of faith and conviction, and to bring victory to Islam by sacrificing his life for the uplifting of Allah's word.[13]

Martyrdom operations have become widespread throughout Arabic and Urdu-speaking Sunni Muslim countries. These attacks by their very nature, as Cook observes, "are really only useful (over the long run) against civilian targets. Military targets are usually prepared for infiltration attempts."[14] These attacks include the killing of infidel women and children, many of whom are Muslim but not considered as such by the radical mindset.

A martyr is believed to have been rendered free from sin by virtue of his or her heroic act. Bin Laden and other radicals glorify martyrdom. Because of their purity, and as a symbol of what they have done, if possible, martyrs are buried in the clothes they were wearing when they died and they are not washed prior to burial. They are entitled to immediate entry into paradise and enjoy special status there. Sura 3:169 says: "Think not of those who are slain in Allah's way as dead. Nay they live, finding their sustenance in the presence of the Lord."[15]

Cook concludes his chapter on "Radical Islam and Martyrdom" with the following observation:

> In the end, the globalist radical Muslim vision of jihad is world domination. Islam must come to dominate the world in its entirety, in accordance with the radical Muslim interpretation of Quran 8:39, "And fight them, so that sedition (temptation) might end and the only religion will be that of Allah." Clearly this absolute vision does not speak for all Muslims, but it does have a resonance for many.[16]

Many wonder why moderate Muslims do not speak out strongly against the radicals. This question will be discussed in more detail later. However, a partial answer to this question is contained in the doctrine known as al-wala 'wa-l-bara (loyalty or disloyalty) which is emphasized almost exclusively by radicals. According to this teaching, Islam is defined by the willingness to fight for Islam and by the polarities of love and hate: love for anything or anyone defined by the radicals as a true Muslim, and hatred for non-Muslims. Anyone who manifests love for what radicals define as a non-Muslim is considered a non-Muslim and therefore by definition is excluded from the Muslim community.

One of the principal reasons for the silence and ineffectiveness of moderate or anti-radical Muslims is the doctrine of al-wala 'wa-l-bara. To oppose the radicals and their definition of what it is to be a Muslim is to risk being considered a non-Muslim. If that occurs, the consequences can in certain cases be dire. Thus, it is impossible in many cases to know, at least publically, what a Muslim really thinks concerning the radical movements.

The question many ask is whether or not radical Islam has a viable future. David Cook, in the Afterward of *Understanding Islam*, argues that it does not.[17] He writes:

> As appealing as fighting and taking revenge for actual and perceived wrongs inflicted on the Muslim community over the past centuries might be, the reality is that jihad during the past two centuries has been a dismal failure, with the possible exception of the expulsion of the Soviet Union from Afghanistan (and that was achieved only with extensive aid from the United States).[18]

Cook does not think radical jihad has a future in the larger Muslim world. He notes that in countries such as Algeria, Egypt, Afghanistan, and Iran, where radical groups have either tried or succeeded in gaining control, there has generally been a strong backlash against their version of Islam. Nevertheless, he does think that radical jihad will continue among marginalized groups and may even gain power "in certain Muslim states of third tier importance.[19]

NOTES

1. Natana J. DeLong-Bas, *Wahhabi Islam* (New York: Oxford University Press, 2004), 3.
2. *Ibid.*, 4, 5.
3. *Ibid.*, 287.
4. *Ibid.*, 288.
5. *Ibid.*, 288-289.
6. Sayyid Qutb, *Milestones* (Karachi: International Islamic Publishers, 1988).
7. *Ibid.*, 64-94.
8. *Ibid.*, 860.
9. Natana J. DeLong-Bas, *op. cit.*, 265.
10. Sayyid Qutb, *op. cit.*, 141.
11. Natana J. DeLong-Bas, *op. cit.*, 265.
12. See David Cook, *Understanding Jihad*, (Berkeley and Los Angeles, California: University of California Press, Ltd., 2005), 142.
13. *Ibid.*, 143.
14. *Ibid.*, 145.
15. Abdullah Yusuf 'Ali, *The Holy Quran*, *op. cit.*, 172.
16. David Cook, *op. cit.*, 161.
17. *Ibid.*, 163-167.
18. *Ibid.*, 164.
19. *Ibid.*, 165.

Chapter Eleven

Western Muslims

TARIQ RAMADAN AND REFORMIST ISLAM

Tariq Ramadan is Professor of Islamic Studies, currently teaching on the faculty of Theology at Oxford University. He is also Visiting Professor at Erasmus University in the Netherlands; Senior Research Fellow at St. Anthony's College, Oxford University, and Doshisha University, Kyoto; and president of the University Think Tank Network in Brussels. He is author of numerous books including *To Be a European Muslim*(1999) and *Western Muslims and the Future of Islam* (2004).[1] Ramadan points out that Muslim communities in the West are living through a veritable silent revolution since more and more young people are actively seeking to live in harmony with their faith while at the same time living in modern secular societies. Beginning with the message of Islam and its universal principles, Ramadan's analysis of Islamic teaching leads to a movement of reform and the manner in which one can integrate into this new environment. It is by acquiring the conviction that they can be faithful to the principles while being totally involved in the life of their societies, Ramadan believes, that Muslims in the West will be able to come to terms with this new situation.

In *Western Muslims and the Future of Islam*, Ramadan writes:

This book is only one step more toward the building of the Muslim personality in the West and doubtless in the modern era too. It will not be the last. Other works, in sha Allah (God willing) must continue to trace the path back to the beginning. I have humbly tried to draw the theoretical and practical outline of a vision of the future, full on. I want to engage with this in practice, and already, across all the countries of the West, this vision is being accomplished. The road is still long, but indwelt by this humble "need of him," one must not be afraid or apologize for needing time.[2]

Ramadan belongs to the Salafi renewal movement begun by Jamal al-Afghani who died in 1887. This movement encouraged Muslims to oppose the colonial domination imposed by Western nations (e.g., Britain, France, Holland) on Islamic countries but did not put the blame on the Western powers for the lack of creativity of the Muslim world. Al-Afghani's movement did criticize the individualism, materialism, and secularism resulting from Western modernity, but its main thrust was on the need for Muslim self-criticism. Al-Afghani argued that the principal reason for the decline of Muslim societies was the stagnation of Islam, its indifference to social inequality, its conservatism, and its suspicion of modern science.

How did the stagnation occur? The answer deals with the collapse of the Abbasid dynasty which ruled the Middle East until 1248, which was the year the destructive invasion of the Mongols took place. The Abbasid dynasty was in power from 750 until 1258. In 1258, Hulagu, a grandson of Genghis Khan, attacked Baghdad and burned the city to the ground. He executed the last Abbasid caliph. The caliphate was transferred to Cairo where it ultimately failed. There was no longer a single voice of authority but Islam continued to expand. Because of cultural pluralism and the absence of a single voice of authority, the ulama became increasingly conservative, fearing the contamination of the teaching of the Qur'an. They believed "the doors of ijtihad" were closed, that is, they rejected new interpretations of the Qur'an which responded to new historical events. This attitude began to change with the reform movement ushered in by Jamal al-Afghani and his followers.

Ramadan presents an example of this stagnation in regard to science. He notes that when the Renaissance, humanism, and the Reformation—all deeply influenced by Islamic civilization—took place in the West, the process of secularization began which "set free the power of reason that has become more and more autonomous and scientific."[3] However, Islamic society did not participate in this process. Muslim scholars preferred to recall the glorious past of Islam regarding science. Ramadan goes on to say:

> Behind this sustained nostalgia and idealized dream, a deep malaise lies hidden, because we do not know, we no longer know, how to realize the connection between religion and science such that religion's ethical teachings give science a dignified finality without perverting its implementation or impeding its advance.[4]

Ramadan goes on to say, regarding scientific challenges, that Muslims must master the rules and methods of the various humanities and pure sciences in order to discuss hypotheses and applications so that they will be able to retain and present a balance between religion and science. This, in turn, will help to discover the reciprocity between the religious and secular understanding of the world.

Toward the beginning of *Western Muslims and the Future of Islam*, Ramadan describes six currents in today's worldwide Muslim community which are important to understand. The distinction often made in the Western media between radical and moderate Muslims does little in providing insight into the complexity of contemporary Islam and its approximately 1.5 billion members. The six current trends are as follows:

1) Scholastic Traditionalism. Those who belong to this group practice their faith by a strict and sometimes exclusive reference to one of the many schools of law. They rely on opinions that were usually codified between the eighth and eleventh centuries. Because they are inflexible in their understanding of Islam, they regard Western modernity as a major threat to their faith. They emphasize obedience to external forms of worship and to dress codes. They believe the door of Ijtihad is closed and any new interpretations of the Quran are seen as baseless and unacceptable. Scholastic traditionalism movements are present in the West, notably in the United States and Great Britain among Indo-Pakistani groups and in Germany among the Turks. They are concerned mostly with religious practice and do not involve themselves in social, civil, or political activities. The exception here is the Taliban.

2) Salafi Literalism. This current strives to practice the Islam lived by the Prophet Muhammad and his "Salafi," which refers to the Companions of the Prophet and pious Muslims of the first three generations of Islam. This current is often confused with scholastic traditionalism although they have significant differences. In contrast to scholastic traditionalism, the Salafi literalists reject the mediation of the juridical schools and their scholars when reading the Quranic texts. Any interpretative reading is forbidden. Only the text in its literal form has binding authority and it cannot be subjected to interpretations that, by definition, contain error or innovation. Wahhabism belongs to this current. These literalists do not look for new insights in the Qur'an that could shed light on the present historical situation. For them, the social environment is characterized primarily by isolation and by a literally applied religious practice protected from Western cultural influences.

3) Salafi Reformism. This approach refers to the Islamic renewal movement begun by Jamal al-Afghani which Ramadan follows. Concerning this movement, he writes:

> They too, therefore, refer back to the Saliphs, the Muslims of the first generations, with the aim of avoiding the commentaries of the eighth-, ninth-, or tenth-century scholars who have been accorded sole authority to interpret the texts. However, in contrast to the literalists, although the texts for them remain unavoidable, their approach is to adopt a reading based on the purposes and intentions of the law and jurisprudence (fiqh). They believe that the practice of

ijtihad (interpretation) is an objective, necessary, and constant factor in the application of fiqh in every time and place.[5]

In other words, Salafi reformism prefers to return to Islam as practiced by Muhammad and his Companions which was open to reason and capable of responding creatively to historical challenges. They maintain that the doors of ijtihad are open so they reread the Qur'an and Sunna (the words and deeds of Muhammad) by taking into account the author's intention. In doing so, they are seeking insights that will cast light on their contemporary experience. But since Ramadan is writing in a pastoral mode, he interprets the Qur'an and Sunna in accordance with hermeneutical principles that are recognized by the Islamic schools of law. He and the reformist movement want to remain faithful to the Qur'an and Sunnah and insist that their rereading of the text, while new, is sanctioned by tradition.

4) Politicized Liberalism. Ramadan refers to this small but highly publicized current as "political Salafiyya." Scholars and intellectuals originally attached to the legalist reformist school went over to strictly political activism usually because they had experienced repression and imprisonment by dictatorial Muslim rulers. They read the Qur'an in a strictly political manner. Their goal is the creation of an Islamic state. As Ramadan notes: "The discourse is trenchant, politicized, radical, and opposed to any idea of involvement with Western societies, which is akin to treason."[6] They call for jihad and opposition to the West "by all means." They plot against Muslim governments that have friendly relations with the West. In *To Be a European Muslim*, Ramadan observes that this grouping represents "less than 0.5% of the Muslim population in Europe."[7]

5) "Liberal" or "Rationalist" Reform. This current is greatly influenced by the values of the Western Enlightenment which grew out of the colonial period and to some extent from the period of the Mutazila, an eighth-century group of theologians, which provided a very open framework and way of reading scriptural sources. The liberals, or modernists, support the application in the Muslim world of the social and political system that resulted from the process of secularization in Europe. They supported Mustafa Kemal's (Attaturk) secularization project in Turkey and promote the complete separation of religion from public and political life. They argue for a complete adaptation of the Western way of life. And as Ramadan states: "They do not insist on the daily practice of religion and hold essentially to its spiritual dimension, lived on an individual and private basis. . . ."[8] They believe modernity calls for a certain break with tradition and believe the legal interpretation offered by the Islamic schools of law has lost its relevance.

The liberals complain that Ramadan's theology and the renewal movement in general defend the authority of the ulama and refuse to recognize the freedom of all believers to read and interpret the Qur'an for themselves. Ramadan believes experts should interpret the Qur'an and that a purely personal reading of the Qur'an is likely to encourage a literalist interpretation. He argues that his position is traditional insofar as the ulama interpret the Quranic verses by taking into account their context and the intention implicit in them. He wants to preserve and promote continuity. He is not a radical. He believes the new insights must be in continuity with the Islamic tradition. It is also noteworthy that Ramadan supports human rights and democratic pluralism in the name of the Quranic faith, but he is not a modernist. For him, there is a significant difference between the renewal movement to which he belongs and liberal Islam.

6) Sufism. Sufism was discussed in an earlier section. As we have seen, it is practiced by many Muslims worldwide. It represents the mystical dimension of Islam. Today, Sufis follow their mystical vocation while observing the rules and external obligations of Islam. Sufi influence also helps many Muslims who are not Sufis to cultivate their spiritual lives.

Ramadan, at the conclusion of his treatment of the six groupings, points out that there are other minor trends of Islamic thought in the West which are too numerous to describe. In sum, his classifications are very useful and make clear that the designations of moderate and radical are anything but accurate in describing and understanding the viewpoints of the approximately 1.5 billion Muslims worldwide.[9]

Some have proposed to call the present situation dar-al-ahad (the land of treaty) since international law and inter-government agreements assure the safety of Muslims in non-Muslim lands. Ramadan sees some merit in this proposition but believes it to be inadequate. He gives several reasons for his rejection of this idea and perhaps the most important of these is that to consider Muslims as citizens, to be in a kind of contract with the "non-Islamic" society, perpetuates the idea that Muslims are not really a part of society but are coming to terms with an entity with which they do not identify. The notion of ahd (treaty) used in this way is quite different from the idea of a "social contract" between a citizen and an entity of which he is a part and in which he feels himself to have full membership.

Ramadan points out that the concepts of dar-al-Islam, dar-al-harb, and dar-al-ahd were not first described in the Qur'an or in the Sunna. In fact, they constituted an attempt by the ulama to describe the world and to provide the Muslim community with a geopolitical scheme that seemed appropriate to the reality of the time. That reality has changed and it has become necessary to go back to the Qur'an and Sunna, and in light of present circumstances, to develop a new vision appropriate to the present time. In fact, millions of Muslims live in Europe and the Americas as loyal citizens and not simply as temporary guests.

LIVING IN NON-MUSLIM SOCIETIES

Muslim schools of law traditionally have made a clear distinction between Muslim and non-Muslim lands. During the early centuries the ulama, considering the geographical divisions and the religious powers that were in place in various regions, classified and defined those areas in and around the places in which they lived. The Muslim regions were called dar-al-Islam (the land of Islam) and the hostile regions dar-al-harb (the land of war). The ulama of the different schools of law did not agree on the definition of these terms. Some thought that dar-al-Islam referred to a place where the population was Muslim, others felt it referred to countries ruled by Muslim law, and others believed it designated places where Muslims were safe and protected. Dar-al-harb referred to areas where Muslims were exposed to dangers and unprotected by law. The schools of law agreed that Muslims could visit these regions but could not settle in them. Ramadan notes that the Salafi literalists still defend the distinction between dar-al-Islam and dar-al-harb and demand that their constituents living in the West isolate themselves from mainstream society.

Today many ulama understand that referring to the non-Muslim world as dar-al-harb is no longer relevant. As Ramadan writes:

> In today's world, where populations are in constant movement in which we are witnessing an increasing complexity in the distribution of economic, financial, and political power, as well as a diversification of strategic alliances and spheres of influence, it is impossible to hold an old, simple, binary vision of reality. That being so, this set of readings is totally inappropriate: it could lead to a simplistic clearly erroneous perception of our times.[10]

Ramadan later writes:

> An environment that guarantees freedom of conscience and worship to Muslims (that is, of their faith and practice), that protects their physical integrity and their freedom to act in accordance with their convictions, is not in fact a hostile space. In North America, as in Europe, five fundamental rights are guaranteed that allow them to feel at home in their country of residence: the right to practice Islam, the right to knowledge, the right to establish organizations, the right to autonomous representation, and the right to appeal to law.[11]

In the present time, Ramadan states, Islam is neither dar-al-Islam, dar-al-harb, nor dar-al-ahd. Rather, Islam is dar-al-dawa (the land of invitation to God). This means that Muslims living in the West, individuals as well as communities, not only may live there but are also bearers of enormous responsibility. They must give their society testimony based on their faith and spiritual values. They must remind the people around them of God and spirituality. They must also be actively involved in supporting social issues based on justice. The responsibility of Muslims, according to Sura 2:143, is "to bear witness (to their faith) before humankind." This is true not only in the West where Muslims live in a pluralistic society, but also in countries whose majority is Muslim. Muslim leaders should provide Western Muslims with appropriate teachings and regulations that will make it possible for them to protect and actualize their Muslim identity, not as Arabs, Pakistani, or Indians, but as Westerners. This slow process has been taking place for more than twenty years and is making possible, according to Ramadan, "the birth of a new and authentic Muslim identity, neither completely dissolved in the Western environment nor reacting against it, but rather resting on its own foundations according to its own Islamic sources."[12]

While respecting the requirements of their religion, Muslims must not neglect the important potential for adaptation that is the distinctive characteristic of Islam. There should be an Islam that is rooted in the Western cultural universe, just as there is an Islam rooted in the African or Asian tradition. Islam is one and unique but its methodologies for its legal application are several and its concentration in a given time and place is by nature plural. This does not mean making concessions on the essentials but rather seeking to remain faithful while allowing for development. In this regard, Ramadan states:

> . . . Muslims should move toward exercising a choice from within the Western context in order to make their own what is in harmony with their identity and at the same time to develop and fashion the image of their Western identity for the present and the future.[13]

Muslims should become good citizens in the Western societies. He reminds Western Muslims that they should stop thinking of themselves as minorities and instead understand themselves as citizens who must make their contributions to the common good and be co-responsible for justice and peace in society, even if at times they have to defend their rights. Ramadan defends the traditional teaching that faith in Islam calls for an active participation in society. With regard to the five pillars, Ramadan maintains that the four pillars (which follow the first pillar, shahadah, by which one becomes a Muslim) are a summons to social solidarity.

1) RITUAL PRAYER, performed five times a day, which is the most important pillar, creates a sense of community among the faithful. The prophet said:
"Communal prayer is twenty-seven times better than the prayer of a man alone
in his house." (Hadith reported by Bukhari and Muslim).

2) ZAKAT. . . . The sense of community is confirmed and reinforced by all the
other religious practices, particularly zakat, which is essentially a tax raised for
the poor and needy.

3) FASTING during the month of Ramadan allows believers to participate in
the hunger suffered by the poor throughout the world. It is time during which
believers strengthen their faith while further developing their sense of social
justice.

4) THE PILGRIMAGE (HAJJ) to Mecca is an important religious experience
which allows one to see the universality of the Islamic community as approximately two million believers from countries worldwide participate in this
religious event. [14]

Islam is clearly a community-oriented faith and for Muslims who live in
the West this means they are called upon to participate in social and political
life in the name of their faith in order to promote the common good. However, one of the key problems for Muslims in the West is the great diversity
within Muslim communities which are the result of identity awareness stem-
ming from different ethnicities and cultures. Ramadan argues that Islam is
not locked into the culture in which it was revealed, but is able to move into
other cultures and to transform them and be transformed by them. And though
Islam has many cultural faces, he insists that Islam is one. In other words,
the many cultural manifestations of Islam celebrate a single Islam which is
divinely revealed.

The ethnic divisions inhibit the Muslim community from being as fruitful
as they might be. Although one might have hoped that having arrived in the
West Muslims would succeed in overcoming their differences of origin, but
the norm is still based on ethnic origin. After decades, there are mosques for
Moroccans, and others for Algerians, for Afro-Americans, for Arabs from
the Middle East, and so on. There are also frequent splits between the social
classes. As Ramadan writes: ". . . it is clearly in the United States that the rift
is most evident between the so-called educated Islam and that of the less af-
fluent, who refuse, usually with reason, to be treated as second-class Muslims
who have not understood the 'wisdom of the message of Islam'."[15] European
Christians went through the same process of assimilation upon their arrival
in America and for the most part have overcome their ethnic differences. In
time, the hope is that Muslims will do the same.

Ramadan defines the identity of Western Muslims without reference to the cultural aspects which were brought by immigrants from various countries. He believes they should define their identity in the following manner in order to overcome division, namely:

1) The spiritual dimension: testifying to the one God, practicing the pillars of Islam, enjoying membership in the umma, and deepening their spiritual life.

2) The intellectual dimension: studying the Islamic tradition, recognizing its contemporary relevance, and being willing to continue to learn.

3) The communicative dimension: passing on the faith to the next generation and explaining the faith to the wider society.

4) The practical dimension: promoting justice in society and serving the common good in other ways.[16]

To attain a strong common identity, Western Muslims must reach a consensus regarding the interpretation of the Shariah. They should cease to follow the ulama from their countries of origin and rely on the ulama who live in the West. What is needed in the West are councils where ulama work together to reach agreements and provide solutions that will be widely accepted and promote unity among Muslims. Two such councils already exist, the Fiqh Council of Islamic Law and Jurisprudence in the United States and the European Council for Rulings and Researches which was founded in London in 1997.[17]

In regard to the question of religious pluralism, Ramadan provides helpful insights. The Qur'an presents a positive interpretation of religious pluralism and the passages cited make clear that such pluralism has been decreed by God for the benefit of humankind. Ramadan quotes the following verses:[18]

1) If God had willed, He would have made you one community but things are as they are to test you in what He has given you. So compete with each other in doing good. (Surah 5:48)

2) If God did not enable some men to keep back others, the world would be corrupt. But God is the one who gives grace to the world. (Surah 2:251)

3) Had God so willed, He would have united them (human beings) in guidance, so do not be among the ignorant. (Surah 6:35)

4) If your Lord had so willed, everyone on earth would have believed. Is it for you to compel people to believe? (Surah 10:99)

5) O people, we have created you from a male and a female, we have divided you into nations and tribes so that you might know one another. (Surah 49:13)

These verses suggest that religious pluralism is God's will and that people from various religious traditions should try to know one another and compete in doing good. But how does one explain the harsh sayings of the Qur'an in regard to Jews and Christians?

There are verses of the Qur'an that describe Jews and Christians, even though they are "people of the book," as infidels or miscreants. A literal reading of various verses leaves little room for discussion in regard to the fate of these infidels. For example, we find in Surah 5:17 the following: "They are certainly in a state of denial, those who have said that God was the messiah, the son of Mary." Other verses include: "Religion in the sight of God is Islam." (Surah 3:19) "He who desires religion other than Islam will not find himself accepted and in the hereafter he will be among the losers." (Surah 3:85) Other verses seem to say the Jews and Christians should not be trusted. For example: "And the Jews and Christians will not be pleased with you unless you follow their religion" (Surah 2:120), and "Let the believers (Muslims) not take as allies the deniers rather than believers: those who do so will receive no help from God, unless you feel yourself in danger from them." (Surah 3:28)

In response to these verses, Ramadan writes:

> The advantage of the literalist reading over all the others is that it stops at the primary reading of the text that, as soon as it is quoted, seems to make immediate sense and gives weight to the argument. No trouble is taken to work out a reading based on critical distance, contextualized interpretation, or determination of the meaning of a verse in light of the message as a whole.[19]

Ramadan rejects the literalist interpretation of these texts because it disagrees with Islam's universal teaching. The idea that religion in the sight of God is Islam suggests to him that whoever surrenders their life to God, in whatever religion, is simply Islamic. The verses that warn against infidels, when placed in their historical context, allows one to see that they were written at times when Muslims were tempted to return to their religious traditions from which they had come. These verses cannot be used to invalidate the more open teaching that religious pluralism is the result of God's gracious design. Ramadan reiterates time and again that the Qur'an contains normative and contextual verses. The normative verses have universal validity and mainly define the believer's relationship to God (e.g., the oneness of God and the five pillars). The contextual verses, referring mainly to social relations, such as those which have been discussed regarding "infidels," must take into account the historical conditions at the time of the writing of the verse in question. If guided by the universal principles implicit in shariah, Islam is capable of addressing all historic situations, including modernity. In fact, the legal tradition of the early centuries allowed it to speak to many different cultures. Ramadan's methodology allows for a critical approach to modernity while maintaining the substance of Islam and rejecting assimilation into secular values. Two issues which Ramadan deals with in this analysis and have yet to be discussed are the role of women in Islam and the question of polygamy.

THE ROLE OF WOMEN

Ramadan recognizes that Muslim women often suffer humiliating subjugation and have to deal with discrimination even in Muslim communities in the West. For many, many Muslims in the West, being faithful to Islamic teachings with regard to education for women, and their access to mosques, marriage, and divorce, social and financial independence, and political participation means doing what was customary in their country of origin. For example, some Muslims in Europe and in the United States do not allow women to enter mosques, and if they do so they are often situated in an area which is dilapidated and without a good sound system. Though this is certainly not the norm, such attitudes still exist in some places.

Ramadan believes the subjugation of women in Islamic societies is a cultural inheritance based on a few verses from the Qur'an and the Sunna. Yet, Islam recognizes the equality of men and women before God. What is happening today is that women have become Islamic scholars and their reading of the sacred texts, their own research, is producing what Ramadan refers to as "the birth of an Islamic feminism."[20] This independent thinking is challenging the cultural inheritance vis-à-vis women. Ramadan maintains that the rise of Islamic feminism is not the result of Western influence. In fact, this movement began with educated women in Egypt who were associated with the reform movement at the end of the nineteenth century.[21]

Ramadan has been criticized for not condemning polygamy nor the right of the husband to divorce his wife by repudiation. Gregory Baum, in his book *The Theology of Tariq Ramadan: A Catholic Perspective*, is probably correct as to why Ramadan has not condemned these practices, namely, because these practices are illegal in the West and forbidden to Western Muslims.[22] Nevertheless, such a condemnation would be welcome. However, Ramadan is certainly clear about cultural practices that place women in subjugation. He writes:

Imams flee "Islamic" justification for "fast-track" marriages, without any pre-paratory official administrative procedures, leaving women without security or rights, abused and deceived by unscrupulous individuals. Divorce is made very difficult when it is clear that the women are defending their most basic rights. Some women, with the knowledge of all around her, suffer violence and deg-radation, while the Muslim community remains culpable, silent and complicit, justifying its inaction and cowardice by reference to the Islamic injunction "not to get involved in what does not concern you." But demanding dignified treat-ment for women has nothing to do with unhealthy curiosity—the first does us honor, the second, to which the Prophetic injunction refers, is unworthy of us. One also finds all sorts of restrictions to do with women, such as the "Islamic prohibition" against their working, having social involvements, speaking in public, and engaging in politics. And what have we not heard about the impos-sibility of "mixing"! It is true that these practices have sometimes been affirmed and advised in the countries of emigration, and one can certainly find ulama in the traditionalist and literalist schools who declare that these are Islamic teach-ings. But it is essential that we go back to the scriptural sources to evaluate these practices (and to draw clear distinction between customs that are culturally based and Islamic principles.)[23]

NOTES

1. Tariq Ramadan, *To Be a European Muslim* (Leicester, UK: The Islamic Foundation, 1999); *Western Muslims and the Future of Islam* (New York: Oxford University Press, 2004).

2. Tariq Ramadan, *Western Muslims and the Future of Islam*, op. cit., 7.

3. *Ibid.*, 3.

4. *Ibid.*, 56.

5. *Ibid.*, 26.

6. *Ibid.*, 27.

7. Tariq Ramadan, *To Be a European Muslim*, op. cit., 243.

8. Tariq Ramadan, *Western Muslims and the Future of Islam*, op. cit., 8.

9. *Ibid.*, 66.

10. *Ibid.*, 66.

11. *Ibid.*, 70.

12. *Ibid.*, 83.

13. *Ibid.*, 85.

14. *Ibid.*, 88, 89.

15. *Ibid.*, 106.

16. Tariq Ramadan, *To Be a European Muslim*, op. cit., 190-195.

17. Tariq Ramadan, *Western Muslims and the Future of Islam, op. cit.*, 202.

18. *Ibid.*, 202.

19. *Ibid.*, 138.

20. *Ibid.*, 138.

21. Cf. Lene Rasmussen, "Muslim Women and Intellectuals in 20th Century Egyptian Debate," The Fourth Nordic Conference on Middle Eastern Studies, Oslo, August 13-16, 1998 (www.hfui3no/snu/pao/kofoed.html).

22. *Perspective* (Notre Dame, Indiana: University of Notre Dame Press, 2009), 133.

23. Gregory Baum, *op. cit.*, appendix.

Chapter Twelve

Gregory Baum: Ramadan and Vatican II: A Comparison

Gregory Baum is a renowned Roman Catholic theologian who was very involved in the Second Vatican Council (1962-1965). He is professor emeritus of religious studies at McGill University in Canada and the author of many books and articles dealing with interreligious relations, including the relation of Catholicism to Islam. His recently published book, *The Theology of Tariq Ramadan: A Catholic Perspective*, presents a comparative approach of the reformist Catholicism of Vatican II and the reform movement in Islam, specifically that movement as situated in the West and exemplified by Tariq Ramadan. The comparison affords a helpful insight into Ramadan's thought.[1] As a young theologian (he is now in his eighties), Baum worked at the Unity Secretariat of Vatican II, which promoted ecumenism and interreligious dialogue and helped to produce the declaration *Nostra Aetate*, which condemned anti-Semitism and purged Catholic teaching of its anti-Jewish bias.

Early in the book, Baum calls to mind what Vatican II said regarding Islam, namely that even though Christianity and Islam are different religions,

. . . the Church regards Muslims with esteem. They adore the one God, living and subsisting in Himself, merciful and all powerful, the creator of heaven and earth, who has spoken to humans; they take pains to submit wholeheartedly to his inscrutable decrees, just as Abraham, with whom the faith of Islam is linking itself, submitted to God....They value the moral life and worship God especially through prayer, almsgiving and fasting. Since in the course of centuries not a few quarrels and hostilities have arisen between Christians and Muslims, this sacred Synod urges all to forget the past and work sincerely for the benefit of humankind, social justice and moral welfare, as well as peace and freedom.[2]

Baum met Tariq Ramadan when he was invited to be a participant on a panel with him. Baum was so impressed by Ramadan's theological ideas regarding the effort to make Islam relevant for Muslims living in the West that he purchased two of his important books, *To Be a European Muslim* and *Western Muslims and the Future of Islam* in order to get a deeper understanding of his thought. He also acquainted himself with various articles on the subject, written by Ramadan.

Baum notes that he has great sympathy for Ramadan's attempt to allow a critical Islamic openness to modernity because the Catholic Church had the same problem until Vatican II reconciled it with political modernity. This latter term refers to separation of church and state, the democratic form of governance, and religious freedom, as well as other rights of citizenship. In the nineteenth century, following the French Revolution, Catholicism remained firmly aligned with the feudal-aristocratic order and strongly opposed the emergence of modern society. This opposition was voiced in a number of papal proclamations, especially in Pope Pius IX's encyclical letter *Quanta Cura* in 1864. Appended to the encyclical was a document entitled "Syllabus of the Chief Errors of Our Times," in which the Pope summarized contemporary church teaching against modern errors. The syllabus was based on a selection of modern errors that had been condemned in some thirty allocations and encyclical letters during the eighteen years of the Pope's pontificate. Some examples of opinions listed as erroneous in the syllabus are:

1) Every individual is free to embrace and profess that religion, which, guided by the light of reason, he or she shall consider true.

2) Humankind may, in the observance of any religion, find the way of eternal salvation and arrive at eternal salvation.

3) The church ought to be separated from the state and the state from the church.

4) In the present day, it is no longer expedient that the Catholic religion should be held as the only religion of the state, to the exclusion of all other form of worship.

5) The Roman Pontiff can, and ought to reconcile himself, with progress, liberalism, and modern civilization.

For many Catholics, this syllabus appeared as a definite divorce of Catholicism from modern civilization. And although there was certainly justification for the syllabus, especially the condemnations it contained of pantheism, naturalism, absolute rationalism, and indifferentism—it did seem that the Pope had declared war on modern society. In 1870, when the First Vatican Council defined papal infallibility, a fortress mentality was assured for many years to come, in fact, until the Second Vatican Council (1962-65).

Since Islam, like traditional Catholicism, sees itself as a total system, Muslim countries challenged by political modernity have defined themselves, as Baum observes, "either as ideologically secular, as Turkey has done, or a religiously reactionary as Iran and Saudi Arabia have done."[3] Ramadan and the reform movement he represents maintain that Muslims are certainly capable of respecting religious pluralism. They recognize that the world we live in has changed, which demands a serious rethinking of previous teaching while at the same time remaining loyal to the essence of Islam. Whether or not their thinking will prevail throughout the Muslim world remains to be seen.

Gregory Baum believes that the Muslim community Ramadan envisages in the West is not a subculture but a denomination. As Baum writes, "A subculture is a collective of people defined by cultural practices that differentiate them from the majority of the population and assign them to the margin of society. This is what Muslim communities in the West often are, but it is not what Ramadan hopes for them. He wants them to be participants in mainstream society."[4]

Baum, in reading Ramadan, believes the latter envisages the Muslim community in the West as a "denomination" rather than as a "subculture." Denominations are entities which are in dialogue with the dominant culture but do not embrace the entire society and represent only a minority. They participate fully in society as active citizens. The Catholic Church did not understand itself as a denomination until the Second Vatican Council and was a religious subculture until then. At Vatican II, the Church accepted and was reconciled with religious pluralism and now cooperates across denominational lines on civic issues. Ramadan desires that Islam should also accept religious pluralism and cease operating as a subculture. If they do so it will allow Muslims to enter into a critical conversation with society as a whole.

Ramadan's theological method manifests an affinity between his openness to modernity and that of contemporary Catholic thought. This is especially true in regard to Ramadan's and Catholicism's social ethics. As Baum points out, both support social democracy, both critique liberal capitalism, both demand a more just distribution of wealth, both encourage the social economy, and both call for solidarity with the poor and with people on the margin of society.[5]

Another similarity between Ramadan's theology and Catholic thought is also found in the defense of tradition that he and Catholic theologians such as Karl Rahner, for example, offer to the more "liberal" thinkers who call for a radical break with tradition. Ramadan embraces Islamic tradition and in studying it finds guidance for his theological position. So, too, do Catholic theologians who study the Bible, the church fathers, and earlier Catholic theologians who deal with modernity in relation to accepted Catholic teaching.

NOTES

1. Gregory Baum, *The Theology of Tariq Ramadan: A Catholic Perspective* (Notre Dame, Indiana: University of Notre Dame Press, 2009).

2. *Nostra Aetate*, in Walter Abbot, ed., *The Documents of Vatican II* (New York: Oxford University Press, 1966), 663.

3. Gregory Baum, *op. cit.*, 26.

4. *Ibid.*, 118.

5. *Ibid.*, 162.

Chapter Thirteen

A Christian-Islamic Dialogue

At a time when the world is increasingly growing together, when the world economy is becoming global, and other religious are not remote entities but close everyday realities, the question is becoming pressing whether the members of different religions, despite their different teachings and rituals, have much to share with one another.

A very important statement was made at the Second Vatican Council in *The Declaration on the Relationship of the Church to Non-Christian Religions*. It reads:

Men look to the various religions for answers to those profound mysteries of the human condition which, today even as in older times, deeply stirs the human heart: What is man? What is the meaning and purpose of our life? What is goodness and what is sin? What gives rise to our sorrows and to what extent? Where lies the path to true happiness? What is the truth about death, judgment and retribution beyond the grave? What, finally, is that ultimate and unutterable mystery which engulfs our being, and whence we take our rise, and whither our journey leads us?

From ancient times down to the present, there has existed among diverse peoples a certain perception of that hidden power which hovers over the course of things and over the events of human life; at times, indeed, recognition can be found of a Supreme Divinity and a Supreme Father too. Such a perception and such a recognition instill the lives of these peoples with a profound religious sense. Religions bound up with cultural advancement have struggled to reply to these same questions with more refined concepts and in more highly developed language.

The Catholic Church rejects nothing which is true and holy in these religions. She looks with sincere respect upon these ways of conduct and of life, those rules and teachings which, though differing in many particulars from what she holds and sets forth, nevertheless often reflect a ray of that Truth which enlightens all men. Indeed, she proclaims and must ever proclaim Christ, "the way, the truth, and the life" (John 14:6), in whom men find the fullness of religious life, and in whom God has reconciled all things to himself (Cf. 2 Cor. 5:18,19).

The Church therefore has this exhortation for her sons: prudently and lovingly, through dialogue and collaboration with the followers of other religions, and in witness of Christian faith and life, acknowledge, preserve, and promote the spiritual and moral goods found among these men, as well as the values in their society and culture.[1]

This statement marks an authoritative change in the approach of Roman Catholicism to non-Christian religions. As long as the world religions, and obviously this includes Islam, were denied the reception of revelation by Christians, dialogue was not seen as useful because all the legitimate claims of the other participants were denied before the conversation began. Now there seems to be an increasing recognition of other religions as entities with which the Church can and should enter dialogue. Such recognition is not found in fundamentalist Christianity.

The traditionalist view of revelation has changed for most mainstream Christian denominations. That view was formulated with great clarity by St. Thomas Aquinas and was held by many Protestant denominations as well as by the Catholic Church. The major division of Christianity's knowledge of God was between natural and revealed knowledge.[2] The "natural knowledge" of God was seen as knowledge that the human mind could attain without any kind of outside help. All the world religions under this scheme would have a "natural" knowledge of God. But however lofty such knowledge might be, it still would not be of saving benefit. At best, so Catholic and many Reformation theologians maintained, it was the knowledge that made humankind "without excuse" in the eyes of God.

But God did leave the human race in this condition. In addition to the natural knowledge of God there is also revealed knowledge. The term "revelation" was denied to natural knowledge because no supernatural aid was required. Revealed knowledge is the truth that is supernaturally communicated to humankind—the truth of the Trinity or the Incarnation of Christ, for example. Three points in particular about the traditional notion of revelation should be recalled:

1. Revelation, in general, was thought of as propositional, and this fitted in well with the Western propensity for exact definition.

2. It was believed that revelation was contained in the Scriptures, and therefore was "possessed." The proof that a revelation had occurred was as external as the proposition itself—namely, miracle and fulfilled prophecy.
3. Finally, the line between natural and revealed knowledge merely separate two kinds of intellectual knowledge. Revealed knowledge was an act of God's grace to humankind. Every person was understood as an *ens Incompletum* (an incomplete being). But nothing in natural knowledge was contradicted by what God had freely added. This notion allowed Roman Catholic missionaries, for instance, to seek points of contact with other faiths, in the assurance that the path to saving knowledge was an unbroken one.

At the turn of the twentieth century, the traditional view of revelation began to break down irreparably. The effects of nineteenth-century theology influenced by biblical criticism, modern science, and the comparative study of religion, all played a part in this break. As long as the distinction between revealed and natural knowledge was allowed to stand, the religions of the world were easily placed by Christian theologians beneath the apex of Christianity. Bereft of revelation they hardly had the nature of religion at all. That Christians, in fact, assumed this attitude of superiority to other religions is easily documented. For example, it was only by a theory of invincible ignorance (it was not their fault) that the salvation of persons outside the Christian fold could be intellectually provided for.[3]

Catholic theologians no longer equate divine revelation solely with Holy Scripture. The highly conceptual understanding of revelation has been superseded, and revelation is now understood as more than propositional truth. From the standpoint of the Christian faith, revelation is now understood as a divine self-disclosure. God does not merely reveal truths about Himself: God reveals Himself to humankind. The church bears witness to, and mediates, this divine self-communication. Although it is still necessary for Christians to hold that the revelation of Christ is final, it is now possible to add, that from another point of view, divine revelation is an ongoing reality among human beings. God continues to communicate Himself to the human race. At the same time, God continues to utter in the Church the Word said once and for all in Jesus Christ. God's present Word evokes the faith of believers now. It is God's continuing self-revelation that creates the Church as the community of believers. Although theological discourse about continuing revelation frightened many theologians of the nineteenth century, today it is quite generally acknowledged that the affirmation of an ongoing revelation in no way weakens the once-and-for-all character of the revelation in Jesus Christ.[4] This shift in the understanding of divine revelation has been acknowledged and accepted by Vatican II in the *Declaration of the Relationship of the Church to Non-Christian Religions* as well as the *Dogmatic Constitution on Divine Revelation* and *The Dogmatic Constitution on the Church.*

The official position of the Catholic Church on the question of the non-Christian religions has passed through various stages throughout its history. There are four historical periods in the development of this teaching. In the first stage, the Church's attitude toward others was primarily negative. Because Jesus was understood as the only mediator between God and humankind, it was taken for granted that the other religions were not salvational. In the second stage, during the medieval period following the First Crusade (1099), the Church felt threatened by Muslim military aggression and the continued presence of distinct Jewish communities. Official Church pronouncements for the first time stated that salvation could only be found in Jesus and the Christian community. In the third stage, which took place in the nineteenth century, the problem was not in regard to other religions but rather concerned liberalism with its egalitarian philosophy that one religion is as good (or as bad) as another. This led to the condemnation of indifferentism.

In the fourth stage, which has only recently emerged after Vatican II, because the reality of religious pluralism struck the consciousness of the Church in a formal way at that council, the teachings of Catholicism regarding non-Christian religions was forced to greatly change.

Many Christians today are aware of the need for a changed and more constructive relationship between the Christian churches and the world's other religions. The obvious beginning of a relationship of this kind is dialogue, and this involves a reciprocal process in which both parties stand on an equal level and are willing to receive as well as to present their own positions. In turn, this means seeing the other religions as in some sense partaking of revelations from God from which Christians can learn. The deeply felt Christian hesitancy about a real commitment to Christ, on the other hand, and true dialogue with other religions, on the other hand, presents a dilemma for many. Such a dialogue is likely to be seen as conflicting with the absolute claims of Christianity. This reaction would be valid not only for fundamentalist Christians but also for many Catholics and other mainline Christians.

Although the right to freedom from coercion in civil society is inviolate, Catholicism obviously has a moral duty to uphold its own self-understanding. At the same time, the Church must be open to all forms of dialogue, be imbued with the spirit of justice and love, and must engage in a common search for moral and spiritual enrichment. Dialogue requires discernment, but it is part of the Church's task and can be done without compromise of its faith in Christ. Pope John Paul II's encyclical *Redemptoris Missio (The Mission of*

Redemption) in 1991 stressed the continued urging of missionary evangelization, and it also commends the need for interreligious dialogue as a part of the church's evangelizing mission.[5] Without abandoning its own principles or promoting false agreements, the Church must enter into dialogue with other religions for the mutual enrichment of the respective communities. The Pope wrote: "Dialogue leads to inner purification and conversion, which, if pursued with docility to the Holy Spirit, will be spiritually fruitful."[6]

It is important to recall that in the past, dialogue with members of the non-Christian religions was even more rare than dialogue with fellow Christians. It was common for most human beings to live their lives in isolation from other major religious traditions, having only a faint interest or awareness in their existence. Often the descriptions of other religions came secondhand and without a true conceptualization. Today, Catholics (and Christians, in general) can no longer ignore other religions. A global religion such as Catholicism constantly meets and deals with members of other faith traditions. It would be wrong to close one's mind and heart to the "other." Without dialogue, fear and misunderstanding can occur, which can lead to hostility and even warfare. In the case of dialogue with members of other religious traditions, there is always the danger of false compromise, but this is certainly not inherent in dialogue. When dialogue is conducted honestly, with full awareness of critical differences, the results can be healthy and fulfilling for everyone involved. This is true even when dialogue involves situations in which one is confronted with what is perceived as genuine evil in the other's attitude or practice. In such an instance, confrontation can lead to an attempt to change the dialogue partner rather than clarifying ideas.

Pope Paul VI, in his first encyclical *Ecclesiam Suam (His Church)*, wrote:

> Dialogue is demanded nowadays. . . . It is demanded by the dynamic course of action which is changing the face of modern society. It is demanded by the pluralism of society, and by the maturity man has reached in this day and age. Be he religious or not, his secular education has enabled him to think and speak, and to conduct a dialogue with dignity.[7]

Vatican II made it clear that dialogue should involve as many persons as possible. The bishops at Vatican II exhorted all the Catholic faithful to take an active part in dialogue, not only with the other Christian churches but also with members of other religious communities such as Islam. This attitude is found throughout the documents of Vatican II as we have seen and was given further standing by the establishment of a permanent Vatican Secretariat for Dialogue with Non-Christians and Non-Believers.

A dialogue partner can become an avenue by which a person or group can perceive itself in a way that could not otherwise occur. In the process of the dialogue and in responding to questions or objections, one gains insights into one's inner self and into one's belief system in ways that might be totally new, and in doing so deepens one's own understanding. This process is analogous to the manner by which one can deepen his or her understanding of their own culture by entering into dialogue with another culture or cultures. This expanded knowledge of one's own faith should lead to a change of behavior, a more open and loving attitude. The purpose of dialogue is not simply to gain knowledge but for all the participants to learn and change accordingly. Christians in dialogue with Muslims and, for that matter, with any member of a non-Christian religion, should first strive to know the dialogue partner as accurately as possible and try to gain an understanding of their beliefs in a sympathetic fashion. Such dialogue should begin by seeking to learn what is shared in common as well as the differences between them. Dialogue should seek to find agreement with one's partner as far as possible on a subject without violating one's integrity. Usually what is shared in common is more extensive than what might have been anticipated. But it is also important to learn what the differences are.

There are many possible subjects of dialogue with Islam such as prayer, fasting, the meaning of law, the Qur'an and the Sunnah, etc. In many ways, the spiritual area is most attractive, at least for those with a more interior or mystical frame of mind. Such an approach promises a great deal of commonality because mystics appear to meet on a high level of unity with the Ultimate Reality, however it is described, including even the more philosophical systems such as Neoplatonism. Using Christian terms, to experience the mystery of God in an authentic fashion is to know with certainty that we are experiencing it only partially. All the major religious traditions seem to agree concerning such religious experience, that God, Allah, etc., can be known only in part. If this is so, then Christians should be open to discovering "other parts" of this mystery. In other words, there is much to learn about the Godhead when understanding how others perceive this mystery.

At present, Catholics and all Christians, as well as all persons of good will, are being called from the age of monologue to the age of dialogue. In the past, it was possible to live in isolation from those who were not part of their community, such as members of the Muslim community for instance. This is no longer the case as we continue to stress. Because of transit and modern communication, large elements of the globe have become present to us. This is certainly true of Islam, which has approximately 1.5 million members. We do indeed live in a "global society." We can no longer avoid "the other," even though we can close our minds and hearts to them and look at them with fear and resentment. But we are called as human beings to true dialogue, to a search for understanding. It is only by struggling out of a self-centered monologue into dialogue with "others" as they really are and not as we have perceived them from afar, that we can really grow. Religions and ideologies must enter into dialogue with full force to help ensure not only mutual understanding and a deeper self-awareness, but perhaps even more importantly a global responsibility that will help make the future one of peace and harmony for all of God's creation. Surely this is the task of the world's two largest religions, Christianity and Islam.

TARIQ RAMADAN: THE NECESSITY OF DIALOGUE

In *Western Muslims and the Future of Islam*, Tariq Ramadan has a section entitled "Toward Exacting and Constructive Dialogue." Addressing Western Muslims, he recommends interreligious dialogue which he believes is a rich educational experience. He describes the beneficial effects of dialogue among believers who belong to different religions by listing four rules which should always be followed. They are:

1. Recognitions of the legitimacy of each other's convictions and respect for them.
2. Listening to what people say about their own scriptural sources and not what we understand (or want to understand) from them.
3. The right, in the name of trust and respect, to ask all possible questions, sometimes the most embarrassing questions.
4. The practice of self-criticism, which consists in knowing how to discern the differences between what the texts say and what our co-religionists make of them, and deciding clearly what our personal opinion is.[8]

Ramadan points out that apart from getting to know one another, it is also necessary to establish relationships of trust and respect. He writes: "Trust is lacking today: we meet often, listen sometimes, and distrust each other often. Trust needs time and support. The frequency and quality of meetings and the nature of the exchanges certainly help to create spaces for sincere encounter."[9] The result of honest dialogue should bring about not only toleration but respect. One truly respects others only by having honest exchanges with them, which leads to the development of better mutual understanding. Ramadan believes that priority must be given to the opening up of minds and hearts: ". . . to be oneself not in opposition to the Other but alongside him, with him, dealing with our differences in active proximity, not in the isolated corners of our intellectual and social ghettos."[10]

In regard to diversity, Ramadan again quotes Sur'ah 5:48: "If God had willed, He would have made you one community but things are as they are to test you in what He has given you. So compete with each other in doing good." Diversity of religions, nations, and peoples is a test because it requires that we learn to manage differences which is in itself essential. If there were no differences between people, if power were in the hands of one group (one nation, one race, or one religion), ". . . the earth would be corrupt because human beings need others to limit their impulsive desire for expansion and domination."[11] The responsibility of humankind is to make use of the differences by establishing a relationship based on excelling one another by doing good. It is critical that such a relationship is based not on mutual ignorance but on a real knowledge of one another. Knowing the other is a process that is unavoidable if fear of difference is to be overcome and mutual respect is to be attained. Dialogue, therefore, particularly interreligious dialogue, Ramadan maintains, is indispensable. And interreligious dialogue should be a meeting of "witnesses" who are seeking to ". . . live their faiths, to share their convictions, and to engage with one another for a more humane, more just world, closer to what God expects from humanity."[12]

Ramadan believes it is very important for the participants in a dialogue to clearly articulate their beliefs, but he feels more is required. It is important, and even crucial, that they describe and explain what they really represent in their religious families—what trend, the extent of it, their relations with the community as a whole, and so forth. He writes:

> It is important to know to whom one is speaking: it is no less essential to know to whom one is not speaking, and why. Interreligious dialogue should make it possible for each partner better to understand the various theories, the points shared, the differences and conflicts that are present in other traditions. It is a matter first of not deluding oneself that the other "represents," for example, the whole of Hinduism, the whole of Buddhism, the whole of Judaism, the whole of Christianity, or the whole of Islam, and second, of knowing what links and types of relations or partners they have with their co-religionists.[13]

Finally, Ramadan maintains that dialogue is not enough. It is only one aspect of the encounter among the various religious traditions. It is urgent that joint social action be practiced. Dialogue allows the participants to realize that they share many convictions and values in common and are often facing the same difficulties and challenges. In philosophical terms, those involved know one another in words but not in action. Ramadan states that his fifteen years of experience of joint action in South America, Africa, and Asia has convinced him that this path is necessary but also that ". . . it is the only way to change minds and build mutual respect and trust."[14] The members of the different religious traditions, such as Christianity and Islam, have to act together so that the body of values that form the basis of their ethics is not relegated to such a private and secluded sphere that it becomes inoperative and socially dead. He concludes his treatment of this issue in the following way. He writes:

> All our religious traditions have a social message that invites us to work together on a practical level. We are still far from this. In spite of thousands of dialogue circles and meetings, we still seem to know one another very little and to be very lacking in trust. Perhaps we must reconsider our methods and formulate a mutual demand: to behave in such a way that our actions, as much as possible, mirror our words, and then to act together.[15]

THE CONTRIBUTION OF HANS KUNG

Hans Kung, in *Islam: Past, Present and Future*, adds another interesting suggestion regarding interfaith relations. He examines whether or not Christians and Muslims, as well as Jews, should pray together. He states:

> If we are clear that Jews, Christians and Muslims serve one and the same God, the question of whether one may pray together is, in principle, easy to answer: people of different religions, and especially adherents of the three Abrahamic religions, may, indeed should, pray together more frequently. There are still considerable differences in thinking about God—even within the Christian communities—but God's reality transcends human understanding and imagining. So a different understanding of God need not prevent shared prayer to the one God.[16]

There is no doubt that such shared prayer is the ideal, ecumenically speaking, but the more difficult question is how this can be done. Despite all that is held in common, there are limits to such shared prayer. Members of a particular religion should not be expected to join in a prayer which expresses the specific prayer of another religion. For example, Muslims would not, and should not, be expected to complete a prayer with the phrase "through Christ our Lord." A great deal of interfaith sensitivity is needed in formulating prayers for shared celebrations. Praying together is an invitation to friendship and is a sharing in the common journey towards the fulfillment of the Kingdom of God. God alone knows what will be possible in the future since Christianity and Islam have just begun to know one another more closely and are taking some tentative steps toward praying together. This has to be true, in fact, within Christianity, where Christians of different denominations are only at present making efforts to come together for prayer. This had not been done since the time of the Protestant Reformation and only had its beginning in the second half of the twentieth century. Certainly there are prayers used in both Islam and Christianity which, with diligence, can be used by both. Kung suggests that new prayers should also be written and he presents a prayer that he has composed that can be used by all members of Abrahamic religious communities. It reads:

> Hidden, eternal, immeasurable God, rich in mercy,
> there is no other God but you.
> You are great and worthy of praise.
> Your power and grace sustain the universe.
> God of truth without falsity, righteous and true,
> You chose Abraham your submissive servant
> to be the father of many peoples
> and spoke through the prophets.
> Hallowed and praised to be your name in all the world,
> and let your will be done wherever people live.
> Living and gracious God, hear our prayer:
> our guilt has become great.
> Forgive us children of Abraham our wars,
> our enmities, our misdeeds against one another.
> Redeem us from all distress and give us peace.
> Guide of our destiny,
> bless the leaders and rulers of the states,
> that they do not lust after power and glory
> but act responsibly for the well-being of their subjects
> and peace among all.
>
> Guide our religious communities and leaders,
> so that they might not only proclaim the message of peace
> but live it out themselves.
> And to all of us, and those who are not of us,
> give your grace, mercy, and all good things,
> and lead us, God of the living,
> on the right way to your eternal glory.[17]

To put Kung's ideas concerning the need for dialogue in perspective, it is helpful to note that in the epilogue of *Islam, Past, Present and Future*, he sketches what he refers to as an image of hope for Islam. He presents a "best-case scenario" an encouraging vision which allows realistic hope for the future and the possibility of dialogue especially in what he refers to as a "global ethic."[18] He says that the decisive question is whether, in some key Islamic countries, they will be able to combine the substance of Islam with the challenges of the twenty-first century. He believes the work of religious reformers is critical since they are opening the door of ijtihad that has been closed for centuries and are undertaking a translation of the original message of Islam for the present day. Certainly Tariq Ramadan is such a reformist thinker.

In regard to politics, Kung states that many Muslims in various countries hope more or less openly that Islam and modern democracy will come together. This has been seen recently and dramatically in Iran. Their desire is to see an end to theocratic clerical rule and the establishment of a democratic system with a separation of powers which would include a government independent of the clergy, and would include independent parties as well as freedom of faith and of conscience. Women should have the same rights as men, which would include involvement in all spheres of public life, in all stages of education, and in all political decisions.

As to religion, Muslims, including reformers such as Tariq Ramadan, take seriously the historical character of God's revelation in the Qur'an and indirectly in the Sunnah (the words and deeds) of Muhammad and in the Shariah. As a result, there should be no fixed literal interpretation but an interpretation which produces a religious heritage in accordance with the spirit and meaning of the whole prophetic book. Kung writes:

> There should be no legalistically overgrown religious heritage but a religious heritage purged in accordance with the criteria of original Islam and reinterpreted for our time. Islam as a foundation should not be understood fundamentalistically but in keeping with our time.[19]

Many Muslims understand that the Arab-Islamic culture has remained fixated on its many past accomplishments and has suppressed all tendencies toward reform and enlightenment which could have led to paradigm changes. As a result, in contrast to European countries, Islamic countries did not develop from trade capitalism to industrial societies. Because of this, there was a complete isolation from scientific, technical, military, and cultural developments. A dependence on European colonial powers, which lasted well into the twentieth century, made the situation worse.

Due to the lack of intellectual freedom in their countries of origin, many Muslim scholars and scientists who did not want to be hampered by existing regimes have migrated to Western Europe and America. Millions of other Muslims, compelled by "circumstances," have joined in this emigration, including refugees from Pakistan, Iraq, Afghanistan, and Iran. The paradigm change that is taking place is not one being imposed by military force as in the period of European colonization, but a more or less voluntary emigration to the West. Because of the freedom experienced in these Western nations, the understanding of Islam living in such a context will probably not result in a literal interpretation oriented on the past but a constructive-reformation interpretation oriented on the future. In this regard, Kung quotes the Muslim scholar Malek Chebel who writes: "One must recall the hope of millions of Muslims who reject a radical Islam (many are even fighting against it at the risk of their lives) and who attach importance to rediscovering a positive Islam, that of Averroes, of critical thought, or the nineteenth century "Renaissance" (nahdah), in a word an Islam of the Enlightenment, an enlightened Islam."[20]

What is important to understand is that the democratic state needs a fundamental ethnical consensus in order to maintain a true sense of freedom. This consensus must be supported by all social groups, to which all religions, philosophies, and world views contribute—in Islamic countries primarily an Islamic consensus, in countries with a Christian character, primarily a Christian consensus. A fundamental ethical consensus is needed, not a "total" consensus but an overlapping consensus on binding values, irrevocable criteria, and basic personal attitudes. It is important that religion does not once again strive for a clerical domination of secular spheres but rather serve to bring about, inspire, motivate, and possibly also correct "secularity" from the perspective of faith. Kung gives three examples of how this might occur:

1) If . . . a majority (of whatever size) says that it will legitimize torture or violently suppress a minority (of whatever kind), then religion must defend the inalienable dignity of every human being and protest.

2) If super-rich potentates shamelessly exploit their people or in a modern business system individual managers dismiss thousands of staff in the name of globalization and vote themselves massive remuneration, then religion may, and should, call for social justice.

3) If a power or superpower thinks that it may unilaterally achieve its aims of hegemony, violate international law, ignore the United Nations and wage a preventive war, then the religious leaders must argue together for peace and against war.[21]

In principle, as Kung notes, the economy, politics, the law, science, the education of individuals, and society need a moral framework. He refers to this as "an ethic of humanity" or a "global ethic." He asserts that Islam, Christianity, and Judaism can make an important contribution to this. Even though often misused, the Qur'an, the Hebrew Bible or the New Testament can give a "global ethic" a solid basis. In this regard, religion is more than just a "subsystem" alongside others. It is interdependent with, and interacts with, all other subsystems as the depth dimension that can always be appealed to in the ethical discourse of a society. Kung believes that a humanistic ethic, with no religious foundation, can also play this social role. To deepen an understanding of a "global ethic" dialogue among these entities is essential.

He adds that a contemporary Islam will not too hastily condemn modernity. On the other hand, there can be no modernistic concessions, no selling out of the substance of Islam. Kung asks of Amr Khalid, a young Egyptian Islamic preacher, represents the model of the future. In contrast to the Ulama, he is modern in his dress (suit and tie), language (Egyptian dialect instead of classical Arabic), and forms of expression (friendly admonitions instead of threats of punishment). He has a large following in the media. He combines Islam, understood in a traditional way, with a modern way of life by emphasizing subjectivity, self-development, and personal responsibility. He does not reject daily prayer, nor abstinence from alcohol, and he teaches a conservative sexual morality. He is not an Islamist nor a member of the old-fashioned Ulama. In answer to Kung's question, it would seem that Amr Khalid, to a great extent, does represent a model of the future.

The problems Islam faces in the twenty-first century are not very different from those of Christianity. There are four problem areas which both have to face, according to Kung, namely:

1) the cosmic dimension: human beings and nature (the concerns of the ecological movement)

2) the anthropological dimension: men and women (the concerns of the women's movement)

3) the socio-political dimension: rich and poor (the concerns of the social organizations)

4) the religious dimension: human beings and God (the concern of the Christian and interreligious ecumene).[22]

Kung concludes his monumental work, *Islam: Past, Present and Future*, by concentrating on the need for interreligious dialogue. He begins by presenting a quotation from the then president of Iran, Seyed Mohammad Khatami, in a speech given to the United Nations General Assembly on September 21st, 1998, where he stated:

. . . Among the worthiest achievements of this century is the acceptance of the necessity and significance of dialogue and the rejection of force, the promotion of understanding in the cultural, economic and political fields, and the strengthening of the foundations of liberty, justice and human rights. The establishment and enhancement of civility, whether at the national or international level, is

contingent upon dialogue among societies and civilizations representing different views, inclinations and approaches. If humanity at the threshold of the new
century and the new millennium devotes all its energy to institutionalizing dialogue, replacing hostility and confrontation with discourse and understanding, it
will leave an invaluable legacy for the benefit of future generations.[23]

The horrific attack on the World Trade Center and the Pentagon on September 11th, 2001, made clear the urgent need for such an initiative as do
the wars in Afghanistan and Iraq and the overall situation in the Middle East.
On November 8th and 9th, 2001, the United Nations General Assembly met
to discuss the question of dialogue between civilizations.[24] After two days of
discussion, the delegates of the various nations, which included many Islamic
states, spoke out against the clash of civilizations and stressed the need for
dialogue among civilizations.[25] Article One of the Resolution describes the
dialogue between the civilizations as a process which is grounded in the
"collective desire to learn, to open up prejudices, and to investigate and develop common meaning and core values." The second article, which is very
important, calls for "the development of better understanding on the basis of
shared ethical standards and universal human values." In this resolution, the
General Assembly expressed the view that there will only be real coexistence
when nations share an ethos and are unified in their commitment to a common good. What the resolution emphasizes is the Golden Rule which is found
in all religions and humanist traditions and calls for awareness, recognition,
acceptance, and celebration of the other in our own self-understanding. Humanity, mutuality, and trust are the basic attitudes which have to be practiced
for a life in the spirit of the Golden Rule.

From the perspective of reconciliation, the resolution lists four irrevocable
directives which, along with the Golden Rule and the principle of humanity,
make up the nucleus of a global ethic, namely: the demands for non-violence,
justice, truthfulness, and the partnership of men and women. Kung briefly
describes these four elementary ethical obligations which are found in all the
great religious and philosophical traditions, are basic in the Qur'an, and are
the Islamic foundation for a global ethic.

1) A culture of non-violence and respect for life is deeply rooted in Islamic ethics. The Qur'an says that the killing of an innocent person is equivalent to killing
the whole of humankind (Surah 5:32). The prophet's concern for animals and
for nature is found in the hadith.

2) A culture of solidarity and a just economic order: Justice is so central in the
Qur'an that only a just person can be a true believer. Surah 5:8 states: "O you
who have attained to faith! Be ever steadfast in your devotion to God, bearing
witness to the truth in all equality; and never let hatred of anything lead you

into the sin of deviating from justice. Be just: this is the closest to being God-conscious." An unjust social order violates Islamic teaching. The Quran requires that surpluses be distributed to the poor and needy. In fact, mandatory alms-giving, the zakat, is one of the five pillars of Islam as we have seen.

3) A culture of tolerance and a life of truthfulness: The ethic of the Qur'an is essentially grounded on faithfulness to the truth. Truth is one of the names of God and is a central value in Islam. A just social order cannot be realized without truthfulness as a fundamental postulate.

4) A culture of equal rights and partnership between men and women. In principle, the Qur'an gives women and men the same status. Surah 2:228 states: "The rights of the wives (with regard to their husbands) are equal to the (husband's) rights with regard to them, although men have precedence over them (in this respect)." [26]

The principle of humanity, which is the most important principle of the global ethic, is found throughout the Qur'an. The golden rule of mutuality is found in the Sunnah: "None of you is a believer as long as he does not wish for his brother what he wished for himself."[27]

All of the above is the common heritage of the three Abrahamic religions and many controversies of the past and present could be overcome in its spirit.

At the end of his book, Kung remarks that the dialogue among civilizations and the idea of a global ethic at the United Nations was stimulated above all by its secretary general, Kofi Annan, who was the winner of the Nobel Peace Prize. Annan believes that universal values are more acutely needed in this age of globalization than ever before because every society is in need of common values so that its members know what to expect from each other and have some shared principles by which to settle their differences without having to resort to violence. Annan argues this is true of local communities and of national communities as well. In his Global Ethic Lecture "Are There Still Universal Values," which he gave at the University of Tubingen on December 12th, 2003, Annan also stated that this applies also to the relationship between West and Islam.[28]

Annan argues that the attack on the World Trade Center must not provoke a "clash of civilizations" in which millions are killed. He emphasizes that the validity of universal values does not depend on their being universally obeyed or applied. Ethical codes are always the expression of an ideal, a standard by which moral failings can be judged rather than a prescription for ensuring that they never occur. For Christianity and Islam, no religion or ethical system should ever be condemned because of moral lapses of some of its members. We need to maintain that certain actions and beliefs are not just contrary to our own particular morality, but should be rejected by all humanity. Having

said this, having such common values, does not solve all problems or elimi-
nate the fact that different societies will solve those problems in different
ways. But at least a foundation will have been laid.

In his brief Conclusion, Hans Kung notes, with a sigh of relief, that he has
completed his trilogy, namely *Judaism* (English translation, 1992), *Christianity* (English translation, 1995), and *Islam* (English translation, 2007). He ends
his work with the following:

> No peace among the nations
> without peace among the religions.
>
> No peace among the religions
> without dialogue between the religions.
>
> No dialogue between the religions
> without global ethical standards.
>
> No survival of our globe without
> a global ethic, a world ethic,
> supported by both
> the religious and the non-religious.[29]

Since peace on earth is the goal of dialogue, it seems appropriate to recall
the words of Pope John Paul II regarding peace. In the decade of the 1980s
and 1990s, the Pope became more and more upset in regard to the economic,
cultural, and military conflicts that were destabilizing global society and
producing massacres in several parts of the world. Reflecting on these issues
in the light of the Gospel, he saw the Church's mission primarily as promoting peace and justice in the world in cooperation with the world religions
and secular ethical traditions. As Gregory Baum observes in *The Theology
of Tariq Ramadan: A Catholic Perspective*, the Pope produced a remarkable document called "Ten Commandments for Peace" which reconciles the
Church to the religious and cultural pluralism of the world and summons all
peoples to seek global peace through dialogue and cooperation.[30] This papal
document is found in the appendix of Baum's book in a section of a letter sent
by Pope John Paul II "to all heads of state and governments" on March 4th,
2002, and reads as follows:

> We commit ourselves to proclaiming our firm conviction that violence and
> terrorism are incompatible with the authentic spirit of religion, and as we con-
> demn every recourse to violence and war in the name of God or of religion,
> we commit ourselves to do everything possible to eliminate the root causes
> of terrorism.

We commit ourselves to educating people to mutual respect and esteem, in order to help bring about a peaceful and fraternal coexistence between people of different ethnic groups, cultures and religions.

We commit ourselves to fostering the culture of dialogue, so that there will be an increase of understanding and mutual trust between individuals and among peoples, for these are the premises of authentic peace.

We commit ourselves to defending the rights of everyone to live a decent life in accordance with their own cultural identity, and to form freely a family of his own.

We commit ourselves to frank and patient dialogue, refusing to consider our differences as an insurmountable barrier, but recognizing instead that to encounter the diversity of others can become an opportunity for greater reciprocal understanding.

We commit ourselves to forgiving one another for past and present errors and prejudices, and to support one another in a common effort both to overcome selfishness and arrogance, hatred and violence, and to learn from the past that peace without justice is no true peace.

We commit ourselves to taking the side of the poor and the helpless, to speaking out for those who have no voice and to working effectively to change these situations, out of the conviction that no one can be happy alone.

We commit ourselves to taking up the cry of those who refuse to be resigned to violence and evil, and we desire to make every effort possible to offer the men and women of our time real hope for justice and peace.

We commit ourselves to encouraging all efforts to promote friendship between peoples, for we are convinced that, in the absence of solidarity and understanding between peoples, technological progress exposes the world to a growing risk of destruction and death.

We commit ourselves to urging leaders of nations to make every effort to create and consolidate, on the national and international levels, a world of solidarity and peace based on justice.[31]

NOTES

1. Austin Flannery, O.P., ed., "The Declaration on the Relationship of the Church to non-Christian Religions," in *Vatican II: The Conciliar and Post-Conciliar Documents*, Vol. 1 (Northport, New York: Costello, 1992), 738-739.

2. Cf. St. Thomas Aquinas, *Summa Theological*, Vol. 1, Q. 12, Arts. 12, 13 (Rome, Italy: Marietta, 1952).

3. Cf. Henry Denziger, *Enchiridian Symbolorun, Definitionum, et Declarationum Rebus Fidei et Morum (Handbook of Creeds, Definitions, and Declarations Concerning Matters of Faith)*. Edited by Adolf Schonmetzer, S.J., 36th Ed., No. 3434 (New York: Herder and Herder, 1976), 1647.

4. See Gregory Baum, The Religions in Contemporary Roman Catholic Theology," *Journal of Religious Thought*, 25(1965):42-43.

5. Pope John Paul II, *Redeptoris Missio, Origins*, Vol. 2, Nos. 3,4 (31 January, 1995).

6. *Ibid.*, No. 56.

7. Pope Paul VI, *Ecclesiam Suam* (Huntington, Indiana: Our Sunday Visitor Press, 1964), No. 78.

8. Tariq Ramadan, *Western Muslims and the Future of Islam, op. cit.*, 210.

9. *Ibid.*

10. *Ibid.*, 110.

11. *Ibid.*, 202.

12. *Ibid.*, 208.

13. *Ibid.*, 209.

14. *Ibid.*, 211.

15. *Ibid.*, 213.

16. Hans Kung, *Islam: Past, Present and Future, op. cit.*, 640.

17. *Ibid.*, 542.

18. *Ibid.*, 644-659.

19. *Ibid.*, 64.

20. *Ibid.*, 647.

21. *Ibid.*, 650-651.

22. *Ibid.*, 652.

23. *Ibid.*, 655.

24. *Ibid.*, 655.

25. Cr. U.N. Resolution A/Res/06/ff. November 9th, 2001.

26. Hadith of an-Nawawi, no. 13

27. Hans Kung, op, citi, 657.

28. Kofi Anna, U.N. Secretary General, in the Third Global Lecture, Tubingen, December 12, 2003, found at www.welthetos.org.

29. Hans Kung, *op. cit.*, 661-662.

30. Gregory Baum, *op. cit.*, 34.

31. *Ibid.*, 171-172.

Chapter Fourteen

Who Speaks for Islam?

Earlier reference was made to the book *Who Speaks for Islam? What a Billion Muslims Really Think*. It makes clear that even in the best of times, American popular understanding of Islam has been informed more by stereotype and suspicion than by reality. Since September 11th, 2001, this sentiment has deepened and a new term, "Islamophobia," has been coined to describe this growing prejudice. On December 7th, 2004, Kofi Annan, mentioned in the last chapter, and at the time Secretary General of the United Nations, convened a U.N. Conference, "Confronting Islamophobia: Education for Tolerance and Understanding," where he stated:

> [When] the world is compelled to coin a new term to take account of increasingly widespread bigotry—it is a sad day for future development. Such is the case with "Islamophobia." . . . Since the September 11th attacks on the United States, many Muslims, particularly in the West, have found themselves objects of suspicion, harassment and discrimination. . . . Too many people see Islam as a monolith and as intrinsically opposed to the West. . . . [The] caricature remains widespread and the gulf of ignorance is dangerously deep.[1]

The catastrophic events of 9/11 and the continued terrorist attacks in Muslim countries, most notably in Iraq, but also in London and Madrid, have increased the growth of Islamophobia almost exponentially. The religion of Islam is regarded as the cause rather than the context for radicalism, extremism, and terrorism. This attitude is short-sided and incorrect. But because of the frequency of terrorist attacks and the hate-filled rhetoric by commentators representing both sides of the issue, which includes both religious and political leaders who speak of an "ideological struggle" between the freedom-loving West and fanatical Islam, have helped foster the view that differences are irreconcilable and an all-out war inevitable.

Numerous negative statements by political types in Europe and the United States have been made. Unfortunately, this is also true of some prominent leaders of the Christian Right in the United States who have demonized Islam. In late 2001, Franklin Graham, the son and successor of Reverend Billy Graham, on NBC News, stated that Islam is "a very evil and wicked religion." In September 2002, the televangelist and founder of the Christian Coalition, the Rev. Pat Robertson, on Fox News' *Hannity and Colmes*, called the Prophet Muhammad "an absolute wild-eyed fanatic. . . . a robber and brigand . . . a killer" and declared that ". . . to think that [Islam] is a peaceful religion is fraudulent." The late Rev. Jerry Falwell, appearing on CBS *60 Minutes* in 2002, called the Prophet Muhammad "a terrorist."

Not all evangelical leaders share these negative views. Dr. Richard Lang, the president of the Ethics and Religious Liberty Commission of the Southern Baptist Convention, condemned these statements by fellow evangelicals. He states: "I disagree with these statements, as do many evangelicals. You know, one of the definitions of a leader is they have followers, and some of the people you've mentioned have fewer followers each year. I thought they [the statements] were erroneous and wrong."[2] Unhappily, Land's remarks did not receive wide media attention.

In *Who Speaks for Islam?*, John Esposito and Dalia Mogahed supplement Gallup's data with articles, reports and analyses of recent events. Their purpose is to democratize a debate that has been dominated by "extremists" and "experts."

Fueling the misconceptions concerning Islam is the tendency to pit a monolithic West—a coherent unit defined by democracy, human rights, gender equality, and separation of church and state—against a monolithic Muslim world with starkly different values. However, Gallup's data refutes this reductive view and reveals commonalities between the two worlds as well as the diversity of Muslim perspectives. Muslims, like Americans, believe attacks on civilians are morally unjustified and are more likely to condemn them unequivocally. For example, 46 percent of Americans, versus 80 percent of Iranians, think that such attacks are "never justified." When asked about dreams for the future, Muslims did not mention jihad but rather the need to find better jobs. Politically, Muslims want neither secularism nor theocracy. They do want democratization but they also believe that society should be based on Islamic values and that Shariah (Islamic law) should be a source of law. Though the fusion of church and state troubles many non-Muslims, it is interesting to note that 50 percent of Americans believe the U.S. Constitution should be based on the Bible. How much shariah should inform legislation varies widely among Muslim nations. In *Who Speaks for Islam?*, some of its most interesting sections discuss these divergent views.

Esposito and Mogahed observe that politics and history, more than re-ligion, explain why democracy is not to be found in much of the Muslim world. The majority of Muslims surveyed support a democratic system, but European colonialism and, more recently, U.S. intervention in the region, including the invasion of Iraq-Afghanistan and the rejection of legitimately elected parties in Palestine, have left many Muslims skeptical of America's democratic agenda.

Skepticism is highest among Islamic political radicals, the 7 percent of Muslims who said they thought the attacks of 9/11 were justified. Contrary to popular opinion, these radicals are not illiterate, impoverished, or homeless. In fact, many of them are well educated (engineers, teachers, physicians, etc.) and are more satisfied than moderates about their financial situations. They are also more cynical about the United States permitting people to fashion their own political future. To diagnose terrorism as a symptom and Islam as the problem, though popular among many pundits, is flawed and has serious risks, according to Esposito and Magahed. Such a view alienates the moder-ates and obscures an evaluation of what, in fact, foments the Muslim/West divide. When asked what could improve relations with their societies, most Muslims advised showing greater respect for Islam and reexamining our in-terventionist policies.

Two events in recent years have sparked Muslim anger in regard to a lack of respect toward Islam on the part of Westerners. In the first event, newspa-per cartoons, including one depicting the prophet Muhammad with a bomb in his turban, were published in Denmark in 2005, and then in other Euro-pean cities. Protests erupted throughout the Muslim world. Newspapers were closed for publishing the cartoons in Jordan, Algeria, and Yemen. Data from the Gallup World Poll serve as a reality check on the causes of the widespread outrage. A major complaint throughout the Muslim world is that the West denigrates Islam and Muslims and equates Islam with terrorism. As Esposito and Magahed point out:

> The cartoons did not satirize terrorists like Osama bin Laden or Abu Musab al Zarqawi, but chose to satirize the venerated prophet Muhammad, whom Mus-lims regard as the ideal model of Muslim life and values, in what was seen as a direct attack on Islam and a denigration of the faith.[3]

Was this response due to the fact that Muslims did not understand or be-lieve in freedom of speech? The Gallup data show this was not the case and show Islamic admiration for Western liberty and freedom of speech. The basic issues here are not democracy and freedom of expression, but faith, identity, respect (or lack of it), and public humiliation. France's Grand Rabbi

Joseph Sitruk observed in The Associated Press in the midst of the controversy: "We gain nothing by lowering religions, humiliating them and making
caricatures of them. It's a lack of honesty and respect." He added that freedom of expression "is not a right without limits."[4]

Unfortunately, the problems surrounding the cartoons was dealt with by
many as a conflict between the absolute right of free speech in the liberal
West and the violent intolerance of the Muslim world, which was not the
case. As Esposito and Magahed write:

> This framing allowed non-representative groups on both sides to monopolize
> the debate and alienate moderate voices on both sides who call for closer rela-
> tions and greater understanding between Muslim and Western communities.
> Inadvertently, the issue played directly into the hands of religious extremists and
> some autocratic rulers who charge that "Western" democracy is anti-religious
> and incompatible with Islam, while giving xenophobic and Islamophobic pun-
> dits yet more fuel to make the same claim.[5]

The second event involves an address by Pope Benedict XVI on September
12th, 2006, at a university in Regensburg, Germany, which triggered an international protest across the Muslim world. Of his eight-page text, only four
paragraphs referred to the Islam. Most offensive to many Muslims was the
Pope's citation of a fourteenth-century Byzantine emperor's remark about the
Prophet Muhammad, namely: "Show me just what Muhammad brought that
was new, and there you will find things only evil and inhuman, such as the
command to spread by the sword the faith he preached."[6] Muslims wondered
why, and were angered, that Pope Benedict would choose to refer to such a
quote.

Another problem emerging from the same lecture was the Pope's statement
that the Quranic passage "There is no compulsion in religion" (Surah 2:256)
was revealed during the early years of Muhammad's prophethood in Mecca,
a time "when Muhammad was still powerless and under (threat)." The Pope
went on to say that this teaching was set aside later when Muhammad ruled
Medina. One hundred leading Muslim scholars and leaders from around the
world wrote and signed an open letter to the Pope that explained several
factual errors made by him in his lecture. For example, they pointed out that
the verse which begins "There is no compulsion in religion" is from the early
period according to the Pope when, in fact, the verse is acknowledged to
belong to a later period of Quranic revelation "corresponding to the political
and military ascendance of the young Muslim community."[7]

Muslims were greatly disturbed that the Pope, the most prominent and influential Christian leader, would apparently denigrate Islam and the Prophet
Muhammad. Although Pope Benedict expressed regret that Muslims were

offended, he did not formally apologize. This exacerbated the situation which began with the Danish cartoons. Commentary on the cartoon controversy and the Pope's remarks were written by Mohammed Reza Jamali in an Iranian newspaper, the *Javan*, and is typical of other such commentaries. Jamali wrote:

> If we look at the situation carefully, we would see that not only is the era of colonialism and all that it entails not over, but amazingly enough of it has come to plunder the material and spiritual resources of the oppressed peoples of the world in a new disguise. The greatest obstacle to colonialism today is the wave of Islamic awakening that has risen from Islamic teachings. It is for this reason that in their new division of labor colonists are targeting Islam and are insulting sacred Islam beliefs.

> The recent offensive statements by the pope and the offensive cartoons that were published a few months ago all serve this very purpose. If Muslims and freedom-loving people everywhere fail to voice their fervent protests and do not condemn these actions, then we predict a rise in this kind of undertaking in the future.[8]

Understanding Muslim sensitivities can be an important aspect in preventing conflict in today's world. Esposito and Mogahed observe that if we place Pope Benedict's speech at Regensburg, as well as the Danish cartoons, within the context of Muslim responses found in the Gallup World Poll data, Muslim reactions are predictable and the conflicts avoidable.

It is important to understand that despite differences, there are a number of areas held in common by the Muslim world and the West. A significant number of Americans and Muslims, according to the Gallup World Poll data, believe that religion is or ought to be a pillar of their society, informed by the Bible or the Qur'an. Majorities in both groups cite the importance of religion in public life and in the preservation of family values. Each group is concerned about its economic future, employment and jobs, and the ability to support its families. Each gives high priority to technology, democracy, the importance of broad political participation, freedom of speech, and social justice. Both strongly support eradicating extremism. At the same time, it is important to note that despite their common Islamic faith, a religion with approximately 1.5 billion members globally, Muslims, like people of many other faiths, have critical theological and political differences and religious orientations that range from the ultra-orthodox to liberal reformers. They are also geographically, racially, linguistically, and culturally diverse. There simply is not a monolithic Islamic religion, anymore than this would be true of Christianity or Judaism.

Unfortunately, Americans have little knowledge of the Islamic religion. When asked what they knew about Islam, the great majority of Americans responded, "Nothing." A first step in overcoming the gap between the West and Islam, between Christianity and Islam, will center on mutual understanding of the other's beliefs. In most instances, this will be done through university and college courses and, as has been discussed, through dialogue. Other sources for mutual understanding will be through seminars at mosques and Christian churches. At the political level, policies must be reevaluated. The argument that a strong military presence will win the war against terrorism is not born out by Gallup data from across the Muslim world. Ultimately, the long war against terrorism will not be won on the battlefield, but by winning the loyalty of the people in the region. Esposito and Magahed write toward the end of their book:

> While terrorists must be fought aggressively, military occupation of Muslim lands increases anti-American sentiment, diminishes American moral authority with allies, and silences the voices of moderates who want better relations. In the end, ongoing conflict between the West and the Muslim World is not inevitable. It is about policy, not a clash of principles.[9]

NOTES

1. Kofi Annan (Kraster, no. 2004, December 10th), "World U.N. Forum Explores Ways to Fight 'Islamophobia'." Retrieved September 18th, 2007, from http:/rfer/org/featurearticle/2004/12/7e9a94e8d-4811-a017-1500 bde 6562.html.

2. Esposito and Magahed, *Who Speaks for Islam?, op. cit.,* 137.

3. *Ibid.,* 143.

4. Barzak, 1, 2006 February 2.

5. Esposito and Magahed, *op. cit.,* 144.

6. Open Letter to Pope Benedict XVI (2006), *Islamic Magazine.* Retrieved from http:www.IslamicMagazine.com/issue18/openletter18-loures.pdf.

7. Esposito and Magaherd, op, it., 149

8. Esposito and Magahed, *Who Speaks for Islam?, op. cit.,* 151-152.

9. *Ibid.,* 166.

Chapter Fifteen

A Cosmic War?

Reza Aslan has written an important and challenging book, *How to Win a Cosmic War*. Aslan is assistant professor of Creative Writing at the University of California, Riverside, and senior fellow at the Orfalae Center for Global and International Studies at the University of California, Santa Barbara. His first book, *No God But God: The Origins, Evolution, and Future of Islam*, has been translated into thirteen languages and was short-listed for the Guardian First Book Award. In his introduction to *How to Win a Cosmic War*, Aslan states that the nineteen men who were responsible for the events of 9/11 were, in their minds, carrying out a liturgical act. They framed the event in cosmic terms as a battle for the sake of God. A document found in the baggage of one of the hijackers contained this statement: "Remember, this is a battle for the sake of God. The enemy are the allies of Satan, the brothers of the Devil. Do not fear them, for the believer fears only God." They had convinced themselves, according to Aslan, that they were serving God by performing their actions. Aslan writes:

> They were engaged in a metaphysical conflict, not between armies or nations but between angels of light and the demon of darkness. They were fighting a cosmic war, not against the American imperium but against the eternal forces of evil.[1]

Aslan points out that a cosmic war is a religious war. It is a conflict in which God favors one side over another. It differs from a holy war which involves two rival religious groups in an earthly battle. Rather, a cosmic war is "like a ritual drama in which participants act out on earth a battle they believe is actually taking place in the heavens. It is, in other words, both a real physical struggle in the world and an imagined, moral encounter in the world beyond.[2]

In a cosmic war, the world is divided into two sides, good and evil. There is no middle ground. Everyone must choose a side. If you are not with us, you are the enemy and must be destroyed. The ultimate goal of a cosmic war is not to defeat an earthly enemy but to conquer evil itself. As a result, a cosmic war involves an absolute, eternal, unending, and ultimately unwinnable conflict.

Those responsible for the attack of 9/11 had many grievances against the United States and the Western world, such as the plight of the Palestinians, U.S. support of Arab dictators, and the presence of foreign troops in Iraq, Afghanistan, and other Muslim countries. But for the Jihadists, these complaints are more symbolic than real. They served not as problems to be solved but as abstract ideas to rally around. The Jihadists are fighting a war they know they cannot win in any real or measurable terms. But they do have a goal, namely, global transformation. But how that transformation will occur and what that new order will look like, the Jihadist ideologues believe need not be addressed until after this world (the evil therein) has been swept away. For the present, they realize they are incapable of reestablishing a world-wide Islamic rule. They will never seize control over the Arab and Muslim world. Nor can they defeat the United States or dispel its influence from the region. They have no hope of "wiping Israel off the map." If the men responsible for 9/11 and their cohorts had a single overriding goal, it was to "unite the Muslim world in the face of the Christian Crusade" and, as Aslan writes, "... to maintain, at any cost, the perpetuation of their cosmic war, for there is no more definite means through which their identity can be sustained."[3]

Very soon after the attacks on the World Trade Center and the Pentagon, the response of many in the United States was to see the war on terror as a Cosmic War. Our identity as a nation was at stake. The world had been split in two, with good on one side and evil on the other. President George W. Bush, an evangelical Christian, promised victory would come only when we "rid the world of evil." Four days after 9/11, President Bush appeared on television, with millions of viewers watching, and stated, "This Crusade, this War on Terrorism, is going to take a while." "Crusade" refers to a "holy war." It was the position that survives to this day, according to James Carroll in *Crusade: Chronicles of an Unjust War.*[4] There is no doubt that this is how a great many Americans understood the term as did many others in the Arab and Muslim world.

In the weeks following, President Bush went out of his way to assure Muslims around the world that he had no intention of launching a crusade against Islam. His advisors explained that he had not used the world in its historical sense. Nevertheless, at the very least, President Bush had ensured that henceforth "this War on Terrorism" would become synonymous with "the Crusade." In doing so, he gave Americans an apocalyptic lens through which to view the coming conflict with the Islamic world and he responded with precisely the cosmic dualism that those who performed the attacks had intended to provoke. As bin Laden said to a reporter a few days after the President's comment:

> Our goal is for the Muslim community to unite in the face of the Christian Crusade . . . Bush said it himself, Crusade. . . . People make apologies for him; they say he didn't mean to say that this was a crusader war, even though he himself said it was!"

And bin Laden continues:

> The odd thing about this is that he has taken the words right out of our mouths.[5]

The Crusades have long been an aspect of the Arab imagination but it was not until the colonial period some eight hundred years later that it became the most powerful symbol of the imperialist aspirations of the West, a kind of shorthand for Christian aggression against Islam. Sayyid Qutb wrote "The Crusader spirit runs in the blood of all Westerners."[6] The connection between colonialism and crusade, and more broadly between Christianity and Western Imperialism, has been etched into the Arab psyche. In many parts of the Arab and Muslim world it is still the principal frame of reference through which relations with the West are viewed.

It is important to stress that for bin Laden and his fellow jihadists, and there are a variety of groups therein, their aim is to attempt to establish a global rule by Islam, a de-territorialized Islam, one unrestrained by the boundaries of ethnicity and culture. From their point of view, the world is divided into two, "the people of heaven" and "the people of hell." There is no middle ground. In a cosmic war, one is either with God or against God. In the words of a member of Algeria's Armed Islamic Group, "There is no neutrality in the war we are waging. With the exception of those who are with us, all others are apostates and deserve to die."[7]

The jihadist practice the use of takfir (excommunication) as was mentioned previously. However, Islam has no means of excommunicating a Muslim. There is not now, nor has there ever been, a centralized religious authority with the power to declare who is and who is not a Muslim. However, the practice of takfir, which traces back to ibn Taymiyyah, places such authority into the hands of individual believers which permits them to declare Muslim enemies to be unbelievers. This allows them to avoid prohibitions against shedding Muslim blood. Jihadists apply takfir to those who disagree with any aspect of their world view. For example, Abu Hamza al-Masri writes in his book, *Beware of Takfir*: "Those who believe in democracy when they vote and they don't mind being elected or to make laws when they have a chance, those people are kaffar (plural of kafir . . . unbelievers). It does not matter how much worship they do or how many times they go on hajj (pilgrimage), they cannot come an inch closer to Islam because of this action."[8]

Down through the centuries, many fatwas (religious decrees) have been given by religious leaders denouncing the practice of takfir as usurping God's dominion. In fact, in 2005, one hundred seventy of the world's leading clerics and religious scholars, who represented every sect and school of law in Islam, met in Amman, Jordan and issued a joint statement. They declared that no Muslim is allowed to label another Muslim an apostate for any reason.[9] The jihadist response to this fatwa was to state that anyone who took part in the Amman Conference was an apostate deserving of death. These Muslim cosmic warriors legitimize their attacks against both military and civilian targets, against both Muslims and non-Muslims, by dividing the world into two separate groups, true Muslims, according to their dictates, and all others. And as Aslan writes:

> They rely on the doctrine of takfir to justify the slaughter of women and children, the elderly and the ill. Although they (e.g., al-Quaeda) are mostly holed up with the remnants of the Taliban in the tribal regions of the North-West Frontier Province on the border between Pakistan and Afghanistan, unlike the Taliban, they have no nationalist ambitions. Their jihad is not a defensive struggle against an occupying power but an eternal cosmic war that transcends all earthly ambitions."[10]

Aslan goes on to say that the U.S. military has had some real success in rooting out and killing the al-Quaeda military. He believes that as an international criminal conspiracy, al-Quaeda is in an existential crisis. Its infrastructure has been destroyed and its rank and file have been almost totally decimated. It no longer possesses the resources it had before 9/11. Its achievements were quite limited. They have not captured a single country. Iraq's Sunni insurgents, who were once their allies, have rejected them due to their disregard for Islam's rules of war. Poll after poll throughout the Muslim world has shown that overwhelming majorities among all classes, ages, and sectors of society condemn their actions. In fact, al-Quaeda's slaughter of innocent civilians and its frequent use of takfir to condemn to death anyone who disagrees with them has turned against them. Even fellow jihadists have turned against them. However, as Aslan writes:

The threat of terrorism from Jihadist groups like al-Quaeda may never fully dissipate. As is the case with any international criminal conspiracy, it may take years, perhaps decades, of cooperation among the military intelligence, and diplomatic apparatuses of nation states around the globe to put an end to Jihadist militancy.[11]

To overcome these insurgents will require more than military might. It will require a deeper understanding of social, political, and economic forces that have made Global Jihadism such an appealing phenomenon, especially to Muslim youth. For many among the young Jihadism is a reactionary identity, a means of social rebellion. It is an identity formed by linking local and global grievances, both real and perceived, "to create a single, shared narrative of suffering and injustice. And only by severing that link, and disrupting the narrative, can Global Jihadism be defeated."[12]

Most importantly, the continued promotion of democracy is critical in that, in the long run, it will bring peace and stability to the Middle East. A patient and aggressive push for greater political participation by all parties in the region will ultimately defeat Global Jihadism because it is precisely that absence of such participation, and the grievances that result, that fuels the movement and keeps it alive. Besides using its military might to destroy Jihadist militants, America must strive to create an open religious and political environment in the Muslim world in order to blunt the appeal of Jihadist ideologies. There are growing demands among Muslims in the Middle East for a voice in government. The need is felt strongly in order, among other issues, to put a stop to arbitrary imprisonments and the silencing of political opponents. What is desired is responsible governance. Substantial majorities in nearly all Muslim countries, for example 95 percent in Burkino, 94 percent in Egypt, and 90 percent in Indonesia, according to the Gallup World Poll, say that in drafting a constitution for a new country, they would guarantee freedom of speech, defined as "allowing all citizens to express their opinion on the political, social and economic issues of the day."[13] However, while admiring many aspects of Western democracy, those surveyed do not favor wholesale adoption of Western models of democracy. Many appear to want their own democratic model that incorporates Shariah, and not one that is simply dependent on Western values. Few respondents associate "adopted Western values" with Muslim political and economic progress.[14]

Another area of interest is the fact that Muslims around the world say that the one thing the West can do to improve relations with their societies is to moderate their views toward Muslims and show respect to their religion. As we have seen, this request for respect is a continuing theme. Since 2002, Gallup pool surveys indicate that a majority of Americans still say they know virtually nothing about the views and beliefs of people in Muslim countries, and for that matter virtually nothing about the teachings of the Islamic religion. Unfortunately, the same is true of the majority of Muslims vis-à-vis Christianity, thus the need of dialogue which, as we have seen, is being urged by many Muslims and Christian leaders.

NOTES

1. Reza Aslan, *How to Win a Cosmic War* (New York: Random House, 2009), 5.
2. *Ibid.*
3. *Ibid.*, 8.
4. James Carroll, *Crusade: Chronicles of an Unjust War* (New York: Metropolitan Books, 2004), 7. See also his essay, "The Bush Crusade," *The Nation*, September 20, 2004.
5. Osama bin Laden, quoted in Bruce Lawrence, ed., *Message of the World: The Statements of Osama bin Laden* (London: Verso, 2005), 121.
6. Quoted in Aslan, *op. cit.*, 204.
7. Quoted in Lawrence Wright, *The Looming Tower: Al-Quaeda and the Road to 9/11* (New York: Knopf, 2006), 190.
8. Abu Hamza al Masri, *Beware of Takfir*, available in English at www.scribd .com/doc/2402521/BewareofTakfir-Abu-Hamza-Almiari.
9. The full text of the fatwa is available in English at http://amneanessage.com// index.php?option-com-content8ctask=view8cid=33/temid=34.
10. Aslan, *How to Win a Cosmic War, op. cit.*, 119.
11. *Ibid.*, 121.
12. *Ibid.*, 153.
13. Esposito and Magabed, *Who Speaks for Islam?*, *op. cit.*, 47.
14. *Ibid.*, 48.

Part III

EPILOGUE

WHY DON'T MUSLIMS CONDEMN TERRORISM?

In his recently published book, *The Future of Islam*, John L. Esposito provides the answer to this question.[1] He notes that the Gallup World Poll discovered that 91 percent of Muslims interviewed believed that the attacks of 9/11 were morally unjustified. As a matter of fact, 358 Muslim employees died in the World Trade Center catastrophe. So many Muslims worked at the Trade Center that a Muslim prayer room had been set aside for them on the second floor of the building. A number of Muslim leaders and organizations did speak out, quickly condemning the attacks, but few media outlets reported their statements and the expression of their condolences. As Esposito writes, "The statements and positions of the mainstream Muslim majority are not headline news, often not even regarded as newsworthy." He goes on to say, "The lack of Muslims' public pronouncements and major statements condemning religious extremism and terrorism has allowed the persistence of the question, 'Why don't more Muslims speak out?'."[2] However, as he demonstrates, this is simply not true. They have spoken out forcefully and often.

Esposito laments that even important political commentators such as Thomas Friedman who is foreign affairs columnist for the *New York Times*, and who had covered the Middle East for six years, on the day after the London bombings in 2005 wrote: "To this day—to this day—no major Muslim cleric or religious body has ever issued a fatwa condemning Osama bin Laden."[3] Even more surprising is the fact that his own newspaper had published a full page ad on October 17, 2001, from the Becket Fund for Religious Liberty which began, "Osama bin Laden hijacked four airplanes and a religion." The ad contained statements by some of the world's most prominent Muslim leaders condemning the attacks. Esposito points out that among those

117

who signed the document were Sheik Abdulaziz, the Grand Mufti of Saudi Arabia and chairman of the Senior Ulama; Zaki Badawi, the principal of the Muslim College in London; Nizamuddin Shaamzai of Pakistan; King Abdullah II of Jordan; and the organization of the Islamic Conference.

Esposito goes on to list other important responses by Muslim leaders which have been basically ignored by the media. Because this is such a vital and even inflammatory question, it is important to list these responses here.

On September 14, 2001, the BBC reported condemnation of the acts of terrorism committed on September 11, only three days earlier. This condemnation was signed by an influential and diverse group of Muslim religious leaders including Sheik Muhammad Sayyid Tantawi, the Grand Sheikh of Cairo's al-Azar University and Grand Imam of the al-Azar Mosque, which is understood by many to be one of the highest authorities in Sunni Islam. Ayatollah Kashani of Iran, the leader of the Shi'ites in that country, was also among those who condemned the attacks.[4]

Another group of over forty Muslim scholars and politicians including Mustafa Mashur, the General Guide of the Muslim Brotherhood in Egypt, and Qazi Hussain Ahmed, Ameer of the Jamaat-e-Islam Pakistan, strongly condemned the attacks. On September 14, 2001, they wrote:

> The undersigned leaders of Islamic movements are horrified by the events of Tuesday, 11 September 2001 in the United States which resulted in massive killing, destruction and attack on innocent lives. We express our deepest sympathies and sorrow. We condemn, in the strongest terms, the incidents, which are against all human and Islamic norms. This is grounded in the Noble Laws of Islam which forbid all forms of attack on innocents. God almighty says in the Holy Quran: "No bearer of burdens can bear the burden of another."[5]

Also, on September 17, 2001, Sheikh Yusuf al-Qaradawi, the chairman of the Sunna and Sira Council in Qatar, and Sheikh Taha Jabir al-Alwani, the chairman of the North American Fiqh (Legal) Council issued a joint fatwa which was signed by American Muslim leaders and internationally prominent Islamic scholars. They condemned bin Laden's attacks of 9/11 and sanctioned Muslim participation in the United States' military response in Afghanistan and stated that every Muslim had a duty to work to apprehend and bring to justice anyone who planned, participated in, or financed such attacks.

Esposito points out that one of the clearest denunciations of terrorism and mindless anti-Westernism appeared in the *Arab News*, a leading Saudi newspaper, shortly after bombings that had targeted Americans in Saudi Arabia in May, 2003. The article stated:

> Words are inadequate to express the shock, the revulsion, the outrage of the suicide bombings in Riyadh. Are expatriates working here an army of occu-

pation, to be slaughtered and terrorized into leaving? . . .We cannot say that
suicide bombings in Israel and Russia are acceptable but not in Saudi Arabia.
The cult of suicide bombings has to stop. So too has the chattering, malicious,
vindictive hate propaganda. It has provided a fertile ground for ignorance and
hatred to grow.

There is much in U.S. policy to condemn; there are many aspects of Western
society that offend—and where necessary, Arab governments condemn. But
anti-Americanism and anti-Westernism for their own sake are crude, ignorant
and destructive. They create hate. They must end. Otherwise there will be more
barbarities.[6]

Many Muslim leaders and organizations continued to respond to every
major terrorist attack such as in London in 2005, Glasgow in 2007, and in
Mumbai in 2008. They globally issued statements condemning the terrorists
and their attacks. For example, Al-Azar's Tantawi stated that the London attacks were the work of "criminals who do not represent Islam or even truly
understand (its message)."

Ayatollah Mohammad Hussein Fadlallah, a prominent Shi'ite scholar,
stated: "These crimes are not accepted by any religion. It is a barbarism
wholly rejected by Islam."[7] Over five hundred British Muslim religious leaders and scholars issued a fatwa in response to the London bombings, express-
ing condolences to the families of the victims. It stated that Islam condemns
violence and destruction of innocent lives and that suicide bombings are
"vehemently prohibited." Surprisingly, for some, Moussa Abu Marzouk, the
political bureau deputy chief of Hamas, stated that "Targeting civilians in
their transport means and lives is denounced and rejected." Hezbollah condemned the London attacks on "humanitarian, moral and religious grounds."[8]

However, as Esposito goes on to say:

Yet the conventional wisdom that Muslims do not condemn terrorism dies hard.
To this day, American audiences still raise this charge despite the fact that Muslim scholars' and organizations' extensive condemnations (including fatwas) of
the 9/11 attacks and subsequent acts of terrorism, issued in countries from Saudi
Arabia to Malaysia to the United States, can be readily found in the international
press and on the Internet.[9]

The reasons for the lack of awareness of Islamic condemnations of terrorism are many. To begin with, the Bush administration's policies fostered
a climate of fear and led to a proliferation of unsubstantiated claims such
as: significant numbers of Muslims in America are terrorists; 80 percent or
more of America's mosques are radicalized.[10] In regard to these claims, a
leaked February 2005 FBI internal memo admitted it had yet to identify a

single al-Queda sleeper cell in the entire United States.[11] Many politicians have added their negative comments to this discussion. Another reason for the lack of awareness of Islamic condemnations of terrorism comes from the demonization of Islam and Muslims by hard-line Christian preachers such as the late Jerry Falwell and Franklin Graham which were previously discussed. Preachers such as these receive a disproportionate amount of attention which obscures many other Christian leaders, churches and organizations that have rejected their hard-line approach and have spoken out for a more pluralistic and balanced approach.

Another important area of concern in regard to the question at hand, namely, an awareness of Islamic condemnations of terrorism, is the media, which generally focuses on crises and amplifies problematic actions in the here and now. It is important that journalists of every stripe keep their civic conscience alert while performing their work. This entails their focusing on processes rather than simply reporting sensational and shocking events. In regard to this, Tariq Ramadan notes that this requires media policies focusing on the training of journalists about religious and cultural issues on the one hand, and social issues and marginalization processes on the other hand. He goes on to say:

> Local media must get involved, and interesting short- and long-term local action must get to be better known. Because they are unavoidable mediators, journalists shape representations and are in effect key protagonists in managing social, religious and cultural pluralism, in developing a sense of common belonging as well as in potentially nurturing fears and phobias."[12]

What is needed are journalists who are willing to contradict accepted opinions and ask appropriate questions. Some few journalists act in this manner but many more are needed. Theirs is a difficult but vital task. Their contributions are essential since they help shape the nature of national and international discourse.

MUSLIM INTOLERANCE—HOW CAN IT BE CONFRONTED?

There are certainly problems with religious pluralism and tolerance in the Islamic world. Religious minorities in Muslim countries often fear the erosion of their rights to equal citizenship and religious freedom—with good reason. Interfaith conflicts have occurred in Pakistan, Egypt, Sudan, Nigeria, Iraq, Iran, Afghanistan, Bangladesh, Malaysia, and Indonesia. Discrimination in these countries is common against non-Muslims, and violence has brought about the destruction of villages, churches and mosques as well as the murder of "non-believers." Many Muslim governments and religious leaders have not done nearly enough to deal with these issues. Those that do deal with the teaching about religious pluralism which are present in the Islamic tradition, reformers, and there are many of them, in dealing with the question of religious pluralism, redefine and broaden traditional theological notions and base their interpretations on the equality of all of humankind, on God's decision to create not just a single nation or tribe, but a world containing different nations, ethnicities, tribes and languages (Suras 30:22; 48:13). The purpose of these differences was not to promote conflict, but rather God's message that all people should try to understand each other and follow God's will.

Abdullah Sachedina of the University of Virginia believes that strict monotheism, Islam's fundamental belief in one God, unites the Muslim community with all humanity. God is the creator of all humans. The Quran teaches that on the Day of Judgment, God will judge everybody on their moral behavior regardless of their religious affiliation. Sachedina states that the belief that "the peoples are one community" is the foundation of a theological pluralism that presupposes the divinely ordained equivalence and equal rights of all human beings.[13]

Among the many reformers, one that should be referred to is Fathi Osman, an Egyptian-American scholar who studied at both al-Azar and Princeton universities. He argues that Islam's religious pluralism is reflected not only in the phrase "children of Abraham," which includes Jews, Christians and Muslims, but also in Sura 17:70 and the phrase "children of Adam," which includes everyone. As a result, Muslim interreligious dialogue should include Hindus, Buddhists, Taoists, and members of other faiths on the basis of Quran's teaching "...that every human being has his or her spiritual compass and has been granted dignity by God" (Sura 17:70). Osman goes on to say that Muslims are not simply to respect others but also have an obligation to guarantee freedom of faith and opinion (Sura 2:256) and freedom of expression to all people (Sura 2:282). Recognition and acceptance of all humanity, all the children of Adam, provides the basis for the development of universal relations and a global ethic.[14]

Sarah Joseph, executive editor of *Emel: The Muslim Lifestyle Magazine*, an influential United Kingdom-based magazine which is circulated in more than thirty countries, makes an interesting distinction between "muslim" and being "Muslim." She explains the distinction between being a "Muslim," that is, anyone who surrenders to God, and "Muslim," that is, a member of the Islamic religion, which is an institutionalized religious entity. She notes that the Quran even describes Abraham as a "muslim." This distinction relates very well with the writings of Sachedina, Osman, and many others, including Tariq Ramadan, whose work has previously been discussed.

John L. Esposito makes an interesting point in regard to American Muslims and their attitude toward religious pluralism. He reports that responses to a question on Islam and religious pluralism in a February 2008 *Pew* survey ". . . demonstrates the pluralistic trajectory of the community. While a minority (33 percent) of those polled responded 'My religion is the one, true faith leading to eternal life,' a majority (56 percent) believed 'Many religions can lead to eternal life.'[15]

REMAINING QUESTIONS

There are many other questions which Muslims will have to answer. For example, are they truly capable of living in secularized societies? Are their values compatible with democracy? Can they live side-by-side and mingle with non-Muslim neighbors? Can they combat the shocking behavior exhibited in their name, in the form of terrorism, domestic violence, forced marriage, and the like? Can they free themselves from their social ghettos? In dealing with these questions, Tariq Ramadan writes that "Muslims must rise to the occasion . They must express confidence in themselves, in their values, in their ability to live and to communicate with full serenity in Western societies."[16] He goes on to say:

> On the social level, we [Muslims] must commit ourselves to a far more social mixing in both our schools and our communities. Far more courageous and creative social and urban policies are needed, of course. But even now citizens can foster human interchange in and through projects focused on local democratic participation. National political authorities must go along with, facilitate, and encourage such local dynamics.[17]

The future of Islam and of Muslim-West relations remains a key religious and political issue in the twenty-first century. Understanding and appreciating shared values and beliefs is critical, especially since 9/11 and all that has followed. This is true not only in multifaith relations but also in international politics. As John L. Esposito remarks:

> Despite the rhetoric and actions of Muslim extremists and terrorists, and religious and cultural differences, the people of America, Europe, and the Muslim world have many shared values, dreams, and aspirations. The future of Islam and the Muslim world is inextricably linked to all of humanity. All of our futures will depend on working together for good governance, for freedom of religion, speech, and assembly, and for economic advancement.[18]

The task presented is incredibly difficult but unavoidable. The peace and security of the world is at stake. It will be the duty not only of religious and political leaders, but of all individuals to participate. If this does not happen, the future will be bleak.

NOTES

1. John L. Esposito, *The Future of Islam* (New York: Oxford University Press, 1020), 29-33.

2. *Ibid.*, 30.

3. Thomas Friedman, "If It's a Muslim Problem, It Needs a Muslim Solution." *New York Times*, July 8, 2005.

4. "Islamic World Deplores US Losses," 14 September 2001, BBC News, http://news.bbc.co.uk/2/hi/Americas/15544955.htm.

5. "Islamic Statements Against Terrorism in the Wake of September 11 Mass Murders," CAIR, http://wwwcair.com/AmericanMuslims/Anti-Terrorism/Islamic-StatementsAgainstTerrorism, ASPX.

6. Editorial, "The Enemy Within," *Arab News* (Jeddah, Saudi Arabia, 14 May, 10 2003, http://www.aljazeerah.info/Opinion%20editorials/2003%Opinion%20Editorials/May/14-b%200/the%Enemy%Within%Arab%News.htm.

7. See "Islamic Statements Against Terrorism" http://www.unc.edu/-Kurzman/Terror.html.

8. Masoud Sabri and Sobby Mujahid, "Muslim Scholars, Countries Condemn London Bombings," *Islam Online*, 7 July, http.net/English/07/o7/articleo7.shtml.

9. John L. Esposito, *The Future of Islam, op. cit.*, 33.

10. See, for example, Haviv Retting, "Expert: Saudis Have Radicalized 80% of US Mosques," *Jerusalem Post*, 5 December 2005, http://www.JPost.com//servlet??/Satellite?cid=11324756899878cpagename=JPost%2fshowfull and Discover the Networks, "Islamic Society of North America (ISNA) 14 February 2005, http://www.discoverthenetworks.org/groupprofile.asp?grpid=6178.

11. "Secret FBI Report Questions Al Quaeda Capabilities," ABC News, 9 March 2005, http://ABCNews.go.com/WNT/investigation/story?id=5664258cpage=1.

12. Tariq Ramadan, *What I Believe* (New York: Oxford University Press, 2010), 78.

13. Abdullah Sachedina, *The Islamic Roots of Democratic Pluralism* (New York: Oxford University Press, 2001), 28.

14. Sarah Joseph, "Text Book Islam," *Emel: The Muslim Lifestyle Magazine*, July 2008, 7.

15. John L. Esposito, *The Future of Islam, op. cit.*, 177.

16. Tariq Ramadan, *What I Believe, op. cit.*, 125.

17. *Ibid.*, 131-32.

18. John L. Esposito, *The Future of Islam, op. cit.*, 199.

Glossary

ADHAN. The call to prayer by the muezzin.

AL-QUAEDA. This term traces back to Osama bin Laden's training camp in Afghanistan. In English it is rendered "the base." The name does not imply that it is the operational seat of global Islamic extremism. At most it is an ideological nerve center propagating a series of propositions that classify the world into Good and Evil. In effect, the name "al quaeda" signifies a movement more than it does an entity.

AYATOLLAH. This translates "A Sign of God." It is the honorary title for high-ranking Shi'ite religious leaders in Iran. There is also an ayatollah in Iraq.

BURQA. In Iran, this is called a chador and it is a full-length garment covering a woman from head to toe.

CALIPH. A political successor of the prophet Muhammad, a leader of the Muslim community.

COSMIC WAR. A Cosmic War is a religious war. It is a conflict in which God is believed to be directly engaged on one side over the other. Unlike a holy war, which is an earthly battle between rival religious groups, a cosmic war partitions the world into black and white, good and evil, us and them . There is no middle ground. If you are not one of us, you are one of them, an enemy that must be destroyed. The ultimate goal of a cosmic war is not to defeat the enemy, but to conquer evil itself.

DAR AL-HARB (literally, "the abode of war"). Territories where Islam does not prevail.

DAR AL-ISLAM (literally, "the abode of peace"). Territories in which Islam and the Islamic religious law prevail, that is, lands under Muslim rule.

DAR AL-AHD (literally, "the abode of treaty"). This term refers to countries that, although not Muslim from a political point of view, have nevertheless signed a treaty of peace and collaboration with one or more Muslim nations.

DAR AL-DAWA (literally, "the abode of invitation to God"). This refers to the responsibility of Muslims to bear witness to their faith before humankind. Muslims in the West should be able to place where they live the "Western abode." The old geographical representation, "the abode of peace" and "the abode of war" no longer bears any resemblance to the spheres of influence in civilization, culture, economics, and subsequently to politics. This term opposes a schema of two "houses" living in confrontation with one another.

DHIMMI. A person who belongs to the category of "protected people" in an Islamic state. In classical times, these were organized monotheists: Jews, Christians, and "Sabians" (monotheists from other religious groups). They were granted autonomy of institutions and protection under Islam. In return, they were required to pay a head tax and an exemption tax. This was usually accompanied by a number of social restrictions. The practice no longer exists.

DU'A (literally, a "plea" or "call"). This refers to calling upon God in supplication or petition. It is spontaneous, an individual prayer, as distinguished from the formal act of prayer, salat. The du'a, whether in group or alone, is performed with the palms of the hands open to heaven. At the end of the du'a the words "praise to God" are said, the palms are drawn over the face and down, crossing over the shoulders. A du'a may be made at any time.

EID AL-ADHA. The feast of the Breaking of the Fast which is celebrated at the end of Ramadan, the month of fasting. This celebration lasts for three days and resembles Christmas in its spirit of joyfulness, special celebrations, and gift giving. In Muslim majority areas, businesses are closed and invitations are extended to family, neighbors, and friends to join in the celebrations.

FATWA. An authoritative legal opinion given by a legal scholar in response to a question posed by an individual or a court of law. A fatwa is typically requested in cases not covered by the legal literature and is neither binding nor enforceable. Present day Muslim states have tried to control fatwas through official consultative organizations within religious ministries.

HADITH (literally, "speech," "report," "account"). Specifically, traditions relating to the words and deeds of Muhammad and the early Muslims. These are considered to be authoritative sources of revelation second only to the Quran. Hadith were collected, transmitted, and taught orally for two centuries after Muhammad's death and then began to be collected in written form and codified. A list of authoritative transmitters is usually included in collections. Compilers were careful to record hadith exactly as received from recognized transmission specialists.

HAJJ. The pilgrimage to Mecca which Muslims are required to make at least once in a lifetime if they are physically and financially able to do so. It is one of the Five Pillars of Islam.

HIGRAH (literally, "the emigration"). This refers to the emigrations of Muhammad from Mecca to Medina at the end of September in 622. In Mecca, the persecution of Muslims had so intensified that the Prophet's life was in danger. He was welcomed to Medina and established the rule of the Muslim community.

HIJAB (literally, "a veil"). A veil covering the hair and head of a Muslim woman. It can also include a long-sleeved flowing dress as well.

'IDDAH. The legally prescribed period during which a woman may not remarry after being widowed or divorced.

IFTAR. The breaking of the fast every evening after sunset during Ramadan. Also, the breaking of the fast of Ramadan on the first sighting of the new moon on the evening of Eid al-Fitr. According to the example of Muhammad, the fast should be broken by eating dates or salt.

IHRAM (literally, "consecration"). The consecrated state entered into to perform the pilgrimage and the name of the garment the pilgrim wears. Ihram is a state of ritual purity and sanctity achieved by renouncing certain activities.

IJMA (literally, "assembly"). One of the principles of Islamic law. It is a consensus, expressed or tacit, on a question of law. It is, above all, the consensus of the religious authorities, but popular consensus is also included in the decision-making.

IJTIHAD (literally, "effort"). The exercise of independent reasoning by a jurist to arrive at a solution to a legal problem.

ISLAM (literally, "submission" or "surrender"). The name of the religion of the Qur'an. One who "surrenders" to the will of God is called a "Muslim."

ISLAMISM. An ideological reform movement that calls for the implementation of Islam in all walks of life, particularly in the social and political realms.

IMAM (literally, "model" or "exemplar"). The prayer leader who delivers the Friday sermon for Sunni Muslims. Shi'a Muslims use the term imam as a title for Muhammad's male descendants through the fourth caliph, 'Ali, and his wife, Muhammad's daughter, Fatimah. Shi'ites believe the imams, although human, were divinely inspired and infalliable, rendering their writings and legal opinions as additional sources of scripture.

IMAN (literally, "faith"). This term designates those articles of belief which are part of Islam. Iman is defined as faith in God, his angels, his books, his prophets, and the Day of Judgment.

ISNAD. A chain of transmitters given at the beginning of a hadith which gives the names of authorities who transmitted the text of the hadith. The authority, and character, including moral probity, of every member of a chain in the transmission of a given hadith, and the existence of alternate chains of transmission for a saying were fundamental criteria for accepting hadith as authentic.

JIHAD (literally, "effort"). An effort or struggle which includes personal striving against sin (the Greater Jihad), and a religious war to prevent or overcome oppression (the Lesser Jihad).

JUMA. The Friday Congregational Prayer.

KA'BA (literally, "cube"). The large cubic stone structure, covered with a black cloth (the kiswah), which stands in the center of the Grand Mosque of Mecca. The ka'ba was originally built by Adam, according to one tradition, and after his death was rebuilt by Abraham and his son Ishmael. Another more accepted tradition believes Abraham and Ishmael were the original builders.

KAFIR (literally, "He who conceals by covering"). The kafir is one who refuses to see the truth, in other words, an infidel.

KALAM (literally, "speech"). Kalam is the term for theology.

KHUTBAH (literally, a "sermon"). This refers to the sermon given at congregational prayer (Juma) on Fridays.

KISWAH (literally, a "cover"). A black cloth which covers the Ka'ba. It is woven of a mixture of silk and cotton and is embroidered with calligraphic inscriptions from the Quran in gold threads in bands around the top. The kiswah also has the Divine Name, Allah, patterned in black-on-black throughout. The kiswah is changed each year and the old kiswah is cut up and distributed to the pilgrims who have made the hajj. While the old kiswah is being replaced, a temporary white covering is placed upon the Ka'ba.

MAHDI (literally, "al-Mahdi" means "the Guided One"). This refers to a person many Muslims, Sunnis as well as Shi'ites, believe will appear toward the end of time, who will restore righteousness briefly—over the span of a few years—before the end of the world. The reign of the Mahdi will be followed by the appearance of the Antichrist who will lead believers away from the truth. Jesus will then come to usher in the final judgment which will be made, not by Jesus, but by Allah.

MINBAR. A pulpit in the mosque used by the imam for preaching the Friday sermon.

MIRRAB. A niche in the wall of a mosque to indicate the qiblah, i.e., the direction towards Mecca, toward which all Muslims turn in prayer.

MOSQUE (literally from "masjid," "a place of prostration"). The prototype of the first mosque is that of the Quba in Medina, which Muhammad built upon his arrival from Mecca.

MUWAHIDDUN (literally, the "Unitarians"). The name by which the Wahhabis prefer to call themselves.

MUEZZIN. One who makes the call to prayer from a minaret.

MULLA (literally, "master"). In Iran and Central Asia, this is a title accorded to religious scholars and dignitaries. It corresponds roughly to the term "faqih" in the Middle East and North America.

MUSLIM (literally "one who submits"). This refers to an adherent of the Muslim faith.

MUSLIM BROTHERHOOD. A religious organization founded in Egypt in 1928 by Hasan al Banna, the grandfather of Tariq Ramadan. It opposes the tendency towards secular regimes in Muslim countries. The brotherhood is the main source of inspiration for many Islamist organizations in Egypt and several other Arab countries. Their tactics have ranged from activities such as caring for the poor and accommodation to political regimes to anti-regime assassinations and violence.

MU'TAZILITES. An eighth-century theological school that emphasized God's absolute uniqueness, unity, and justice. They rejected anthropomorphism and preached harmony between human reason and revelation.

QIYAS (literally, "measure" or "exemplar"). In Islamic Law, the deduction of legal prescriptions from the Quran or Sunnah by analogical reasoning.

QUR'AN (literally, "reading" or "recitation"). The holy book of Islam. It is the primary source of doctrine in Islam. The Qur'an is divided into 114 chapters, each of which is called a surah.

QURAYSH. A tribe located in Mecca. The prophet Muhammad was a member of the Banu Hashim clan of the Quraysh tribe.

RAK'AH (literally, "a bowing"). This refers to one complete cycle of sacred words and gestures during the ritual prayer. It includes standing, bowing, prostrating, and sitting. Each of the five daily prayers is made up of several such cycles.

RAMADAN. This is the ninth month of the Arab and Islamic calendar. Fasting during this month is one of the Five Pillars of Islam.

SABIANS. A people named in the Qur'an (2:59; 22:17), along with Jews, Christians, and Zoroastrians as having a religion revealed by God. The concept of the Sabian was an open door for toleration to any religion which, upon examination, appeared to be an authentic way of worshipping God.

SALAT (literally, "prayer," "worship"). This is the second Pillar of Islam referring to the prayer required of Muslims five times daily: at daybreak, noon, midafternoon, sunset, and evening.

SAWN (literally, "to fast"). The Prophet Muhammad recommended fasting as a spiritual discipline. In addition to the fast during the month of Ramadan from dawn to sunset, there are many optional fast days in the Islamic calendar.

SHAHADAH (literally, "to testify" or "to witness"). This is the first and most important of the Five Pillars of Islam. One states: "There is no God but the one God and Muhammad is the messenger of God." By such testimony, one accepts Islam and becomes a member of the community.

SHARI'AH. This is the canonical law of Islam as given in the Quran and the Sunnah and elaborated by the analytical principles of the various schools of Law. The Quran contains only about ninety verses directly and specifically addressing questions of law. Islamic legal discourse refers to these verses as God's law and incorporates them into legal codes. The remainder of Islamic law is the result of jurisprudence (fiqh), human efforts to codify Islamic norms in practical terms and legislate for cases not specifically dealt with in the Quran and Sunnah.

SUFISM. This refers to Islamic mysticism. The Arabic word "suf" means "wool" and refers to the rough woolen clothing worn by the early ascetics who preferred its symbolic simplicity to richer and more sophisticated materials. Sufism's goal is the direct knowledge and union with God. Its doctrine and methods are derived from the Quran and Islamic revelation.

SUNNAH (literally, "custom"). The predominant meaning of Sunnah is that of the words and deeds of the Prophet Muhammad and other early Muslims which are found in the Hadith.

SURAH (literally, "a row"). This refers to a chapter in the Quran. In all, there are 114 suras.

TAKFIR (literally, "an unbeliever"). This refers to a pronouncement that someone is an unbeliever (kafir) and no longer a Muslim). This has become a central ideology of various militant groups but Muslims generally reject the idea of takfir as un-Islamic and marked by bigotry and zealotry.

TALIBAN (literally, "the students"). In 1994, the movement known as the Taliban arose in the area of Kandahar (Southwestern Afghanistan) and began to take control of Afghanistan. The Taliban took the city of Kabul in 1996, and by 2000 it controlled the entire country with the exception of the province of Badakhshan. The Taliban were originally composed of war orphans educated in schools which taught a form of radical Islam. Strictly speaking, they are not part of the globalist radical Muslim movement but were and are very sympathetic to the movement. For example, they allow Osama bin Laden to take refuge in Afghanistan and later in Pakistan.

TAQLID (literally, "imitation"). This refers to strict conformity to legal precedent, traditional behavior, and doctrines. This is often juxtaposed with ijtihad which refers to independent reasoning based on revelation. In law, taqlid is the reliance upon the decisions and precedents set in the past.

TARIQAH (literally, "path"). This term refers to a "school" or "brotherhood" of mystics of which there are many. Such Sufi orders follow the regimen of a specific teacher or master which includes devotional practices. Every group has its own *dhikr* ("remembrance"). *Dhikr* may be an act of individual devotion but the term usually refers to collective devotions whose specific formulas and prayers are used by the tariqah and identifies the group.

TAWHID (literally, "to acknowledge oneness"). Tawhid is the defining doctrine of Islam. It declares absolute monotheism—the unity and uniqueness of God as creator and sustainer of the universe.

ULAMA (literally, "learned"). This refers to those who are recognized as scholars or authorities of the religious sciences, namely the imams of important mosques, judges, teachers in the religious faculties of universities, and, in general, the body of learned persons competent to decide upon religious matters.

UMMAH. This term refers to the entire Muslim community throughout the world.

WUDU. This is the obligatory cleansing rituals performed to render the believer ritually pure. It is required for prayer for both men and women and consists of washing the hands, mouth, face, arms up to the elbows, and feet. Water is usually poured over the top of the head as well.

ZAKAT (literally, "purification"). This is the required alms-giving which is one of the Five Pillars of Islam. Muslims who are financially able are required to give 2.5 percent of their net worth annually. Zakat is used for the needy, for the propagation of the faith, to free slaves, to relieve debtors, and to help travelers and for other uses approved by religious authorities.

ZAMZAM. The name of the well near the Ka'ba discovered by Hagar after she and her son Ishmael had exhausted the water in the goatskin given them by Abraham. Hagar ran seven times between two small hills looking for water. This action is reenacted each year during the pilgrimage. Pilgrims drink water from this well as part of the ritual.

Further Reading

Ali, Yusuf A. *The Koran: Text, Translation and Commentary.* Washington, D.C.: American International Printing Company, 1946.

Armstrong, Karen. *Islam.* New York: Random House, Inc., 2000.

Aslan, Reza. *No God but God: The Origins, Evolution and Future of Islam.* New York: Farrar, Strauss and Giroux, 2007.

———. *How to Win a Cosmic War.* New York: Random House, 2009.

Barrett, Paul M. *American Islam.* New York: Farrar, Strauss and Giroux, 2007.

Baum, Gregory. *The Theology of Tariq Ramadan: A Catholic Perspective.* Notre Dame, Indiana: University of Notre Dame Press, 2009.

Bonner, Michael. *Jihad in Islam History.* Princeton, New Jersey: Princeton University Press, 2006.

Carroll, James. *Crusade: Chronicles of an Unjust War.* New York: Metropolitan Books, 2004.

Cole, Juan. *Engaging the Muslim World.* New York: Palgrave Macmillan, 2009.

Delong, Natana J. *Wahhabi Islam.* New York: Oxford University Press, 2004.

Esposito, John L. *Islam: The Straight Path.* New York: Oxford University Press, 1988.

———. *The Future of Islam.* New York: Oxford University press, 2010.

Esposito, John L. and Dalia Magahed. *Who Speaks for Islam?* New York: Gallup Press, 2007.

Denny, Frederich Mathewson. *An Introduction to Islam.* Upper Saddle River, New Jersey: Pearson Education, Inc., 2006.

Heck, Paul L. *Islam, Christianity and Religious Pluralism.* Washington, D.C.: Georgetown University Press, 2007.

Karabell, Zachary. *Peace Be Upon You.* New York: Alfred A. Knopf, 2007.

Kalidi, Tarif. *The Muslim Jesus.* Cambridge, Massachusetts: Harvard University Press, 1993.

Kung, Hans. *Islam: Past, Present and Future.* Oxford, England: Oneworld Publications. English Edition, 2007.

Lewis, Bernard. *Islam and the West.* New York: Oxford University Press, 1993.

Ramadan, Tariq. *To Be a European Muslim.* Leicester, U.K.: Islamic Foundation, 2001.

———. *Islam, the West, and the Challenges of Modernity.* Leicester, U.K.: Islamic Foundation, 2001.

———. *Western Muslims and the Future of Islam.* New York: Oxford University Press, 2004.

———. *Radical Reform.* New York: Oxford University Press, 2009.

———. *What I Believe.* New York: Oxford University Press, 2010.

Ruthven, Malise. *A Fury for God: The Islamists Attack on America.* London: Granta, 2002.

———. *Islam in the World,* 3rd Edition. New York: Oxford University Press, 2006.

Saeed, Abdullah. *Islamic Thought.* New York: Routledge, 2006.

Index